Earth-Friendly Desert Gardening

Earth-Friendly Desert Gardening

Growing in Harmony with Nature
Saves Time, Money, and Resources

Cathy Cromell, Jo Miller, and Lucy K. Bradley

Illustrations by Janice Austin
Cover Design by Tamara Kopper

Arizona Master Gardener Press
in cooperation with The University of Arizona
Maricopa County Cooperative Extension

Publisher's Cataloging-in-Publication
(Provided by Quality Books, Inc.)

Cromell, Cathy.
    Earth-friendly desert gardening : growing in harmony
with nature saves time, money, and resources / Cathy
Cromell, Jo Miller, and Lucy K. Bradley ; illustrations
by Janice Austin ; cover design by Tamara Kopper. -- 1st
ed.
    p. cm.
    Includes bibliographical references and index.
    LCCN 2002095633
    ISBN 0-9651987-4-X

    1. Desert gardening--Southwest, New.   I. Miller,
Jo, 1955- II. Bradley, Lucy K. III. title

SB427.5.C76 2003   635.9'525'0979
                          QBI02-200820

Issued in furtherance of Cooperative Extension work, acts of May 8 and June 30, 1914, in cooperation with the U.S.
Department of Agriculture, James A. Christenson, Director, Cooperative Extension, College of Agriculture & Life
Sciences, The University of Arizona.

Table of Contents

Acknowledgements

The authors would like to thank the Arizona State Land Department and the Arizona Community Tree Council, Inc. for awarding a Community Challenge Grant to publish this book. We appreciate the assistance of Ron Romatzke, State Land Department, and Louise Wakem, ACTC, in coordinating the grant. We are also gratefully acknowledge Janice Austin and Tamara Kopper for their artistic contributions as illustrator and cover designer, respectively. Many people shared their experience and assisted in the creation of this book and we appreciate their input and support:

Louisa Ballard, Volunteer Coordinator, ASU Arboretum
Robert H. Bettaso, Native Fish Program Manager, Arizona Game and Fish Department
Jim Christenson, Associate Dean & Director, College of Agriculture & Life Sciences, University of Arizona Cooperative Extension
Frederick J. Deneke, Visiting Professor, USDA Forest Service, School of Renewable Natural Resources
Donna DiFrancesco, Water Conservation Specialist, City of Mesa
Stan Farlin, County Director, Maricopa County Cooperative Extension
Roberta Gibson, Entomologist
Dawn Gouge, Urban Entomologist, University of Arizona Cooperative Extension
Val Little, Water Conservation Alliance of Southern Arizona
César Mazier, Director of Horticulture, Desert Botanical Garden
Terry Mikel, Commercial Horticulture Agent, University of Arizona Cooperative Extension
Thomas Ogren, Author
Mary Kay O'Rourke, Associate Professor of Public Health Research, University of Arizona College of Public Health
Selby Saubolle, Poco Verde Landscaping
Karen Schedler, Heritage Environmental Education Manager, Arizona Game and Fish Department
Maricopa County Cooperative Extension: Carolyn Chard, Joanne Littlefield, Kathleen Moore, Cathy Munger, Carol Noyes, Cathy Rymer
Maricopa County Master Gardeners: Copper Bittner, Marianna Hancin, Shanyn Hosier, Marjorie Sykes, Annette Weaver
Thomas Thompson, Associate Soils Specialist, University of Arizona Cooperative Extension
Joe Yarchin, Regional Urban Wildlife Specialist, Arizona Game and Fish Department
Members of the Summer 2002 Maricopa County Master Gardener class, including Lee Ann Aronson, Pat Briscoe, Carole Flores, Terah Galati, Iris Graeber, Evan Hammond, Clifford Hirsch, Bill Johnsen, Fred Krafcik, Debora Life, Lois Markis, Ruthann Raitter, Jo Setliff, Maryann Taliaferro, Anne Tiernan, Alice Trujillo, Barbara Vietor, Sue Walde, Neva Wuerfel, David Yehling.

My special thanks to entomologist Roberta Gibson, whose extensive comments on integrated pest management and help in locating and identifying insects photos were invaluable. I am also grateful to Carole Palmer for her ever-diligent and good-humored production assistance.

—*Cathy Cromell*

Brad Lancaster and Tim Murphy gave me information on the concept of using solar arcs through a variety of discussions we have had over several years. Scott Frische and Tim Murphy have shared a wealth of experience on site assessment and reading the land. Vicki Marvick and Brandy Winters have shared and encouraged within me the insights to make my dreams of sustainability a practical part of my life.

—*Jo Miller*

Many thanks to the Master Gardeners of Maricopa County, Arizona, whose commitment to sharing information on earth-friendly gardening has inspired this book.

—*Lucy K. Bradley*

Introduction

As our population continues to grow, we become more aware of the impact our choices have on our world. As we live closer together, our personal decisions about how to care for our yards have more impact on our neighbors. Even though we may have less property to manage, the consequences of our choices are increasingly important.

The good news is that individual homeowners can make a real difference in our surroundings. It is possible to have an earth-friendly yard that conserves water and energy while attracting native wildlife and providing a bountiful harvest. All that is needed is a commitment to the environment and some basic information. *Earth-Friendly Desert Gardening* provides strategies in six areas to help you manage your yard harmoniously with nature:

- ✓ Energy Conservation
- ✓ Water Conservation
- ✓ Green Waste Reduction
- ✓ Water Quality Preservation
- ✓ Wildlife Habitat
- ✓ Edible Landscaping

Energy Conservation. As energy prices escalate, we become more concerned about how to conserve. Two-thirds of household energy use is for heating and cooling, which we can reduce up to 60 percent by selecting the right plants and placing them appropriately in the landscape. These same principles of energy efficiency will also extend the period we can enjoy outdoor living areas.

Water Conservation. Landscapes guzzle up to one-half of all water used by a household. In summer, 60 to 80 percent of water use may go towards the landscape. We can reduce water consumption by up to 50 percent by careful planning, plant selection, and plant maintenance.

Green Waste Reduction. Each person in Arizona generates an average of 5.9 pounds of solid waste daily, sending over 2000 pounds per year to the landfills. More than 30 percent of the material is organic matter that we could reuse as compost and mulch in our gardens and landscapes. This would reduce the amount of green waste trucked to the landfills by 600 pounds per person per year.

Water Quality Preservation. Urban water run-off accounts for the majority of water pollution that does not come from a specific industrial source. Overused and/or misapplied pesticides and fertilizers in home landscapes are a primary cause. Selection of well-adapted plants, effective pest management, and appropriate care and feeding of plants can greatly reduce dependence on fertilizers and pesticides.

Wildlife Habitat. Wild habitat areas around cities and even smaller communities are rapidly being converted into housing and commercial properties, displacing native plants, animals, and insects. Choosing native plants for the landscape can create a haven for butterflies, birds, lizards, and other animals.

Edible Landscaping. In our society there is a huge gap between food consumption and food production. Many children, when asked where carrots come from, will reply "the grocery store." They have no concept that the orange vegetable they eat was once the root of a plant growing beneath the soil. Many of the varieties of fruits and vegetables available in our local markets were grown thousands of miles away. To ensure that it is in pristine shape for the consumer, produce is bred for increased shelf life rather than improved flavor or increased nutritional value. By choosing to grow some of our own food we can help our children and neighbors develop a connection to food as a plant, rather than as a package from the store. We can reduce the amount of resources spent on packaging, storing, and shipping produce by harvesting our own salad for dinner. Making the commitment to eat produce grown on our property will profoundly impact our decisions on how we care for the land.

In addition to all the global benefits outlined above, there are specific, personal benefits to earth-friendly gardening:

Save Money. Earth-friendly desert gardening can generate great financial savings on electric bills and water bills. You will also spend less on fertilizers, pesticides, and yard maintenance.

Save Time. Reduce the amount of time spent pruning, mowing, fertilizing, and managing pest problems.

Grow in Harmony. Make decisions in your yard that are healthy for you, your family and pets, your plants, birds and other wildlife that visit your yard, as well as your community.

Grow Your Own Food. Enjoy fresh, sweet-tasting homegrown produce.

This book provides specific strategies on how to become a more efficient consumer and more responsible steward of the land. It includes techniques to save you time and money while creating a positive impact on the environment. Information is presented in the same sequence as the typical gardener would need it, starting with Site Assessment and progressing through Landscape Design, Plant Selection, Plant Maintenance, and Integrated Pest Management. If you are particularly interested in one aspect of earth-friendly gardening, such as creating a wildlife habitat, checklists in the Appendix will guide you through the possibilities.

Small changes can make big differences. Use *Earth-Friendly Desert Gardening* to simplify your life while fostering beauty and harmony in your yard.

Chapter 1

Site Assessment

Imagine giving someone directions to your house without using street names or names of buildings to guide them. To accomplish this, you would have to be knowledgeable about natural landmarks and characteristics of your "bioregion." A bioregion is generally defined as an area whose rough boundaries are formed by natural elements rather than by human decree. It is distinguished from other regions by its flora, fauna, soil, water, climate, and land forms, as well as human settlements and cultures that have evolved in conjunction with these natural elements.

How does knowledge of your bioregion relate to landscape design? Ideally, your earth-friendly desert landscape will function in cooperation with its larger bioregion. How you preserve or restore the integrity of your bioregion depends upon how you perceive the land and the sense of place that you develop over time. Creating a landscape design that integrates into the larger bioregion is no accident. Careful observation, knowledge about your area, and awareness of common patterns in nature are all essential. To design with this natural integrity in mind, you will need to perceive, preserve, and create habitat for people, plants, and animals that encourages them all to thrive. To accomplish this, an investment in a larger vision is crucial.

Many of the ideas in the first two chapters in this book are derived from permaculture design principles. The term "permaculture" was coined in the 1970s by an Australian ecologist named Bill Mollison. Permaculture is a method of designing sustainable human environments based on the observation of natural systems, the wisdom of traditional methods, and the appropriate use of modern science and technology.

Permaculture is an ethical system stressing positive action based on cooperation with the earth. It incorporates the following three themes, which will be explained in greater detail in the next chapter. They can provide a framework for contemplating and developing your own larger vision for your landscape.

✓ *Care of the earth: Preserving natural systems.* This includes all living and non-living things, such as animals, plants, land, water, and air. Patterns in nature form systems that ultimately form an intricate web of life.

✓ *Care of people: Promoting self-reliance and community responsibility.* This requires recognizing that we are a part of the natural world and we make choices that impact the balance of life.

✓ *Investment in the future: Living within our ecological means.* This means recognizing our limits, sharing surplus, and making sustainable choices with future generations in mind.

Assessing Your Landscape

Site assessment allows the landscape to "have a voice" in its design. During this process, your needs and

Benefits of Site Assessment

Save money by placing plants where they will help cool or heat your home and thus reduce energy bills.

Save money by selecting plants that will not need to be replaced or constantly cared for.

Restore degraded landscapes, buildings, soils, and species resulting in greater economic, environmental, and cultural wealth.

Enjoy a harmonious and productive landscape without wastes or toxins.

Belong to a cooperative and information-rich regional society.

Make a measureable contribution to the greater good. Examples: Produce 10 percent of the food your family consumes; Reduce water run-off from the site to less than 25 percent; Develop a system to use 50 percent of household graywater in the landscape.

Create a landscape that requires less energy inputs (water, fertilizer, time, money) and less work to maintain.

Share your insight about the bioregion with others.

your vision can be reconciled with the needs of the land. A well-conceived site assessment will provide the following:

✓ A baseline or foundation for all subsequent work.
✓ An archive of information about your site to help make future design decisions.
✓ An understanding of the natural energies (sun, wind, rainfall) present on your site and how to integrate those energies.
✓ An easy-to-follow design process that collects information vital for water conservation, energy conservation, green waste reduction, water quality preservation, and wildlife habitat.
✓ The opportunity to grow some of your own highly nutritious food.
✓ An interconnected design allowing more intricate and beneficial relationships between people, plants, and animals to emerge.
✓ A more sustainable landscape requiring less plant replacement and less long-term care and maintenance.
✓ A sense of what is culturally appropriate for your area.

Begin your site assessment by spending time outside and paying attention. Take some time to get to know your landscape and your region. Learn to listen to the land with all of your senses. The practice of listening to the land invites you to learn to live *with* the natural world rather than exert dominion over it. If you are new to your bioregion, be patient. You may need several years to develop and install an integrated design. Follow the lead of many experienced gardeners who consider their landscapes as "works in progress." Often the temptation exists to make a place into something you are familiar with as opposed to what actually is appropriate for your area. "Forcing" a design to happen leads to struggling plants, excessive water and fertilizer applications, wasted resources, and an empty wallet. Once you become a member of a neighborhood, it is your responsibility to care for that land in such a way that you enhance the ecological community of the area.

Landcare History

An important part of site assessment is to explore the land's history. Many design questions can be answered and creative ideas stimulated by looking at the history of the site. Find and informally interview neighbors who are long-time residents, read historic accounts on the area, and visit local museums, botanical gardens, and historical societies. The answers to the following questions will give you many clues to what is appropriate for your home's ecosystem and will help develop your sense of place:

❑ What was here (plants, animals, landforms) before my house?

❑ What is the history of landcare since my house was built? Before my house was built?

❑ What cultures have evolved in this area?

❑ What has been their relationship with the land? How did they use water? What crops did they grow? What time of year did they plant?

❑ What landcare issues are present in my area today? Is native habitat disappearing? Is erosion a concern? What about the water supply?

Observing Patterns in Nature

Careful observation leads to identifying repeatable patterns occurring in nature. Examples of common natural patterns include spirals (galaxies, pine cones, DNA), branching patterns (trees, river deltas, tributaries), and flow patterns (how wind or water flow around an obstacle). Patterns are also observed in the form of energy (sun, wind, rain, human) flowing through a system. For example, wind may flow in a linear, circular, or spiral pattern. The goal is to apply the observation of patterns to a landscape plan that is harmonious with these patterns rather than in conflict with them.

As an example, consider a large, man-made site such as a college campus. Sidewalks are usually laid out in straight lines and grids. However, humans seldom walk from place to place in a square "traffic" pattern. Instead, we follow a "branching" pattern (similar to the flow of rivers and tributaries) that takes us to our destination by the easiest or shortest route. This is why trampled grass and shortcuts through the shrubbery are so often seen in many large-scale human developments. Natural patterns were not taken into account during the design process. Recognizing the traffic patterns, both human and animal, on your own landscape will be one part of your site assessment.

Try to look at your landscape as an ecology where everything works together. The challenge is to position and interconnect all the elements in the system in beneficial relationships to each other. Consider what would happen if there was nobody to maintain your landscape. Would it survive? A design becomes more sustainable when it provides for its own needs by creating a diverse system of connections. For example, rainwater can be directed to fill a pond that provides water for birds. A small saguaro cactus benefits from the shade of a so-called "nurse" tree. As it outgrows this need, both plants can provide food and shelter for native wildlife. Composting recycles organic matter back into the garden, releasing nutrients for another cycle of plant growth.

Mapping the Site

Start by drawing a sketch of the site. Indicate what direction is north. Draw and label any permanent buildings or structures. This is your base map. Then begin observing natural patterns and energy flows such as sun, wind, traffic patterns, slope of the land, and rainfall. Take mini vacations in your yard. Spend 30 minutes a week (all at once or spread out over the week) observing what naturally happens in your yard and in your neighborhood. Add these energy flows to the base map as

The sustainable garden is modeled on nature. Nature works upon the basis of patterns in many dimensions; it is no accident that rivers curve, or that bees build honeycomb hexagons. Learning from observation of nature shows us that patterns are the way to build strong and enduring systems.
—The Permaculture Garden

you observe them. Specific factors regarding sun, wind, and the other energy flows, as well as considerations for fire and lightening, are discussed in the following sections.

The Sun

Strategically located landscape plants can reduce air conditioning costs significantly, according to the U.S. Department of Energy. Planning a landscape for energy conservation requires an understanding of sun exposure and seasonal angles. The position of the sun differs from summer to winter. During summer, the sun is high in the sky, moving almost directly overhead. This creates very short shadows at noon. On Summer Solstice (about June 22), the sun reaches its highest angle in the sky. In winter, the sun drops lower in the sky toward the south. This angle creates very long shadows at noon. On Winter Solstice (about December 22), the sun is at its lowest angle in the sky.

On your map, mark the sun angles at the Winter and Summer Solstice. Note any buildings or structures that may cast long shadows in the winter caused by the low angle of the sun. In the summer when the sun moves to a more overhead position, those same areas may receive little to no shading. Make a note on your map of any areas with seasonal shading.

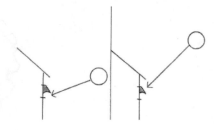

(Above) Window awnings can be positioned to block the higher summer sun while allowing the lower winter sun through to warm the house.

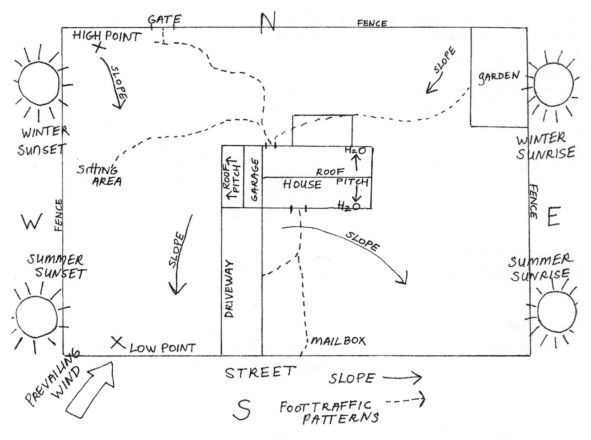

A sample site assessment that includes directions, sun angles through the seasons, prevailing wind, high point, slope and roof pitch (for harvesting rainwater), and regular foot traffic.

When you understand how the sun hits your landscape at certain times of the year, you can use "passive-solar" methods to capture and direct energy. Passive-solar techniques position plants and other landscape elements in specific locations to reduce heat and glare. These methods help heat and cool buildings, provide and modify microclimates for plant growth, and moderate temperatures in outdoor living areas.

A simple but very effective passive-solar technique is the use of a "solar arc," which is a protective planting that creates a heat trap in the winter and a cooling effect in the summer. This type of planting is sometimes referred to as a "heat sink" in colder climates. Brad Lancaster, who teaches and writes about permaculture in Tucson, Arizona, coined the term solar arc to emphasize its more important role in moderating the sun's heat in the desert Southwest.

Solar arcs are created by planting trees and other vegetation in an arc from east to north to west around a specific structure or feature. It may be a continuous arc of plants, or it may consist of several smaller adjoining arcs. A solar arc can also be created with mounds of soil or with a combination of plants interspersed on soil mounds. For example, soil mounds might be two feet tall planted with species that can live on natural rainfall such as prickly pear, cholla, jojoba, or desert willow. Plants and trees requiring additional water could be placed in basins created from making the mounds. You may want to consider planting deciduous trees for the east and west sides of the arc. These trees provide shade in the summer. When their leaves drop in winter, the low angles of the sun's rays are allowed through to warm your home. The concept of planting in arcs can also be applied to create windbreaks.

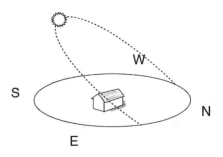

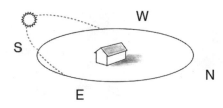

(Top) In summer, the sun is high in the sky, which creates very short shadows at noon.

(Bottom) In winter, the sun is low in the sky, which creates longer shadows at noon.

Note that the position of the sunrise and sunset in the winter is farther south in the horizon than in the summer, when the sunrise and sunset are positioned farther north in the horizon.

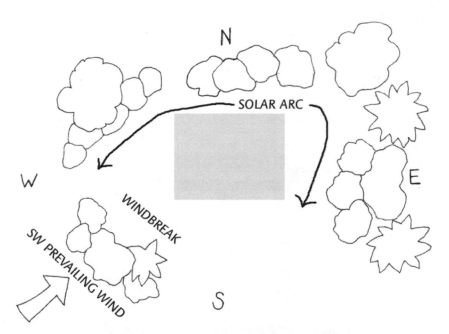

Planting in an arc around the home from east to north to west creates a heat trap in winter when the sun is low in the southern sky and the rays reach the home. It provides a cooling effect in summer when the sun is high in the sky and plants block the rays.

Another energy-saving method is to provide shade close to the south side of your house, which is exposed to the sun the longest in the summer. This can be accomplished with either vines or some type of appropriately sized roof overhang or a patio or ramada cover that allows full sun in the winter but blocks out the summer sun. For example, vines can be trained to grow vertically up a trellis providing shade for a south-facing window. They can also grow horizontally over the top of a ramada. Deciduous vines work well for this, providing shade in summer and allowing winter light through. To create cover, you might erect shade cloth over a patio or put an awning on a window. Awnings should be positioned to allow winter sun to reach the house, but block summer rays.

Wind

Most desert gardeners are aware of our intense sun and the need for appropriate irrigation. An often overlooked element of desert landscaping is the wind. It can have a very significant drying effect in the garden in summer as well as hot spring and fall days. In winter, the wind can bring chilling air to frost-tender plants. In the desert environment, three aspects of wind should be considered:

✓   The drying effect of hot, summer winds.
✓   The destructive impact of monsoon thunderstorm winds.
✓   The chilling effect of cold, winter wind.

Hot summer winds. Typically, the prevailing wind in much of the Southwest comes from a southwesterly direction. This generally is a hot, drying wind that can intensify if it travels upslope. When buildings or other large obstacles (such as fences or walls) are close together and one structure is blocking the path of the wind, a tunneling effect may occur. This situation can change the direction of winds across your property. Additionally, the wind velocity may increase and swirling patterns can occur. Pay attention to wind patterns on your property and include them

A trellis planted with vines at the south side of a building provides shade, reduces energy use, and extends outdoor living space.

Earth-Friendly Gardeners

Pima County Master Gardeners sheltered south-facing walls and windows of the Cooperative Extension building in Tucson. They built a simple metal arbor and planted grapevines to create a shady retreat covered with lush vines in summer. "The windows provide a close-up view of birds and ground squirrels seeking shade and fresh grapes," describes Master Gardener Linda Drew. The vines die back in winter, allowing the sun to warm the building. A few years later, the Master Gardeners added hardscape features and container gardens to complete the oasis, creating a sanctuary from a once-unappealing space.

on your map. Place a large arrow pointing in the direction of the typical wind patterns or the prevailing wind for your area.

Monsoon winds. Because the direction of monsoon winds is so unpredictable, it is difficult to erect effective windbreaks. If trees do blow over during a monsoon storm, you can use their direction of fall as an indicator of possible monsoonal wind patterns for your area.

Cold winter winds. Generally, cold winter air moves in from the north after a winter storm disturbance. Cold air moves much the same way as water flows, traveling downslope and settling in the lowest spots. Have you ever walked through a wash on an evening hike and felt an incredible drop in temperature? This is a dramatic example of how cold air will collect in low spots. Vertical obstacles such as walls, fences, and dense vegetation can also block or trap cold air. Cold air may settle in such an area, creating a frost pocket. It is best not to plant frost-sensitive plants (non-native tropicals such as bougainvillea, citrus, ficus, hibiscus, jacaranda, natal plum) in an area you identify as a frost pocket. Instead, this may be a good spot to plant deciduous fruit trees, such as apple trees, that require a chilling factor. If frost-sensitive plants already exist in such an area, a solar arc made from plants, soil mounds, or a combination of the two can help protect them from the movement of cold air.

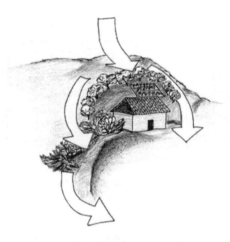

Cold air sinks, providing a chilling effect where it settles. Windbreaks can direct the air around the house.

Most landcapes and gardens could benefit from some type of wind protection, usually from the prevailing wind. Planting trees, shrubs, or vines on the side of the garden exposed to the prevailing wind will help in normal wind conditions and reduce the need for excessive watering. This should be sufficient for average wind conditions.

The term "windbreak" usually brings to mind a long, straight line of tall trees stretching along the perimeter of a property. However, there are other styles of windbreaks that are better suited to specific situations. If your property is located toward the top of a wind-facing slope, in an area of wind tunneling, or in a low-lying area prone to frost, you may want to

Planting trees and shrubs perpendicular to the prevailing wind will reduce household energy use and the need for excessive landscape watering. Some of the wind will go through the plants, but the majority will go up and around.

consider any one of the following types of windbreaks. The Plant List in the Appendix contains suggested plants for windbreaks.

Alternating arcs. A windbreak with alternating arcs of trees is placed throughout the landscape. These are sometimes referred to as "in-garden" windbreaks because they are located within the property rather than along the edges. The trees should have a multi-trunk, open branching pattern with an airy canopy, which allows wind to pass through easily, as opposed to a single-trunk tree with a dense, tight canopy. Most desert trees, such as palo verde, ironwood, and desert willow, fit this profile. In addition to reducing wind velocity, an in-garden windbreak increases humidity and provides shade and forage for wildlife.

Permeable hedgerow. A permeable, low hedgerow allows the wind through while reducing its velocity. The goal is to slow the wind down, but not stop it, which can create dangerous localized gusts. Use prickly pear, jojoba, small acacia trees, desert willows, or other small trees or shrubs that can take the wind.

Plants of various sizes. Alternately placed windbreaks using plants of various shapes and sizes works on a very large site, with the plants spaced throughout the area.

Low-growing permeable plants allow the wind through, while reducing its velocity.

Traffic Patterns

Wildlife. Wildlife corridors often exist even in highly developed urban areas. These corridors may include areas that specific animals or groups of animals move through for hunting, foraging, and drinking. These corridors may also provide a passage to seasonal habitats and/or feeding and mating grounds. This movement of wildlife provides balance in nature, increases the diversity of the natural world, and helps prevent vegetation in one area from becoming overbrowsed. If you live in an area bordering different habitats, you may experience more species more frequently. On your map, indicate any areas where you have noticed that animals routinely frequent or any pathways and green corridors they may be using.

People and Pets. Begin observing and mapping human traffic patterns on your property, as well as pet activity. Be sure to indicate routine movement patterns such as taking out the trash, walking to the compost bin, getting tools from the tool shed, going to the garden to harvest herbs, or playing with the dog. If you would like your yard to be an extension of your living space, begin thinking of pathways, stepping stones, sitting areas, and similar elements that invite people to come out and walk around.

Slope and Drainage

In most urban situations, rainwater is managed by directing it to storm drains constructed to run "perpendicular to contour"—a term engineers use for what the rest of us simply call downhill. This results in water moving quickly downslope to retention areas or streets. The result is that little or no water penetration occurs in the soil, especially in the desert's hardpacked, sunbaked environment. Salt accumulates in the soil because water doesn't penetrate deeply enough to leach it away. Erosion and flooding may occur if there is a high volume of water or it is moving rapidly. Additionally, "non-point source pollution" may be increased as moving water carries contaminants with it. Non-point source pollution comes from many sources rather just one site, such as a factory. (Landscape maintenance practices that help reduce this type of pollution are discussed in Chapter 4.)

On gently sloping land, you can encourage water penetration and storage in the soil by constructing simple earthworks, such as mulch pits or swales. They also cool surrounding areas and promote healthy vegetation. Mulch pits, swales, and other types of earthworks are described in Water Harvesting Methods later in this chapter. Small or large properties, with or without a detectable slope, can use earthworks to encourage water penetration. On steeper slopes, terracing is the preferred method of water harvesting and erosion control.

When assessing slope for your site map, also consider your house and other structures as "hills" or "mountains" where water is running down their "slopes" when it rains. Because slope and rainwater are interconnected, marking them on your site map will be combined in the next section.

Rainwater

The largest volume of water on most urban lots collects as runoff from the roof of the house and other structures. The Sonoran desert receives 7–14 inches of rain annually, depending on elevation. In a typical "rain event," less than one-half inch falls, but a two-inch rain event is possible. Even with this small amount of rainfall, an amazing amount of water can be collected as roof runoff from an average home. Most people are surprised at the volume of water that can be collected in one rain event.

Most urban lots are designed to drain the roof runoff into the streets. This method treats the rainwater as undesirable by diverting it off the property as quickly as possible. With a little planning and with the use of some simple water harvesting techniques, the same water can become a resource used to water plants, leach the soil of salt build-up, and/or fill a small pond.

Collecting rainwater is not a new concept. For hundreds of years, humans diverted precious rainfall or stored it in clay pots and gourds for later use. A few generations ago, cisterns were a common feature of rural homesites, and many people saved rainwater in wooden barrels strategically placed below the eaves. Much of the modern canal system that has fostered the dizzying pace of Arizona's urban development traces the same irrigation paths that early Native Americans dug to direct water to their crops.

A benefit of rainwater harvesting is reduced erosion in the natural washes. "With increasing development, there are more paved surfaces in our cities," explains Cado Daily, Program Coordinator for the University of Arizona Cooperative Extension's Water Wise Program in Sierra Vista, Arizona. This creates heavy runoff and tremendous erosion in the washes. Harvesting rainwater that falls on our properties helps control that erosion.

How to Calculate the Amount of Rain Runoff from Rooftops*

Information Needed

✓ Roof area in square feet (length by width).

✓ Annual rainfall in feet (divide your area's average annual rainfall in inches by 12).

✓ Conversion factor to change water from feet to gallons (7.48).

✓ Runoff coefficient (.90). It will be impossible to collect 100 percent of the rain falling on your roof. This runoff coefficent allows for some loss due to splash and evaporation.

Formula

(roof area in square feet) x (annual rainfall in feet) x (conversion factor) x (runoff coefficient) = potential gallons of annual rainwater.

Example

Roof: 50 feet long x 20 feet wide = 1000 square feet.

Rainfall for Phoenix area averages 10.8 inches per year. 10.8/12 = .9.

1000 x .9 x 7.48 x .90 = 6058 gallons.

* Adapted from *Harvesting Rainwater for Landscape Use*, Patricia H. Waterfall, University of Arizona Cooperative Extension/Low 4 Program.

We take for granted that we can turn on a faucet to water our landscape, but many parts of the country have been experiencing drought conditions. Restrictions on landscape watering have been imposed in such diverse regions as Maryland, California, and Colorado. Harvesting rainwater can keep your plants alive during a drought. The more ways you can provide water for your landscape, the more sustainable it will be.

Harvesting rainwater involves collecting rain as it runs off a "catchment" surface and directing the water elsewhere, either to a specific area in the landscape or to a storage container. The most efficient catchments are smooth hard surfaces where water flows easily, such as rooftops, paved driveways, sidewalks, and patios.

To add relevant information to your base map for slope and rainwater, observe how water currently flows and/or collects on your property. On your base map:

- ❑ Indicate with arrows the pitch of the roof and the flow of water from the roof.
- ❑ Indicate the high point and the low point of your property.
- ❑ Make note of any areas where water flows on or near your property from an outside source.
- ❑ Mark any areas where water tends to accumulate.
- ❑ Indicate the direction and approximate degree of slope of the property.

Water Harvesting Methods

If you are constructing a new home, a complete water harvesting system can be designed to make maximum use of the desert's limited rainfall. For example, create a slight slope to impermeable surfaces such as concrete driveways and sidewalks so that water flows off into landscape areas rather than rushing into the street. Where possible, use permeable surfaces for paths, patios, and driveways to allow water to soak into the ground. Situate rain barrels in areas where they are less visible or add screening features so they aren't noticeable. Consider the slope of your lot and include "earthworks" in your landscape design. Earthworks slow

Advantages to Using Rainwater in the Landscape

✓ Rainwater is better for most plants. It has lower salinity than municipal water. Rainwater can help dissipate and leach salts from root zones. This means there is less salt build-up in the soil and plants are less likely to suffer the yellowing and browning foliage caused by salt burn.

✓ Less rainwater is lost to evaporation if it is absorbed by the soil, rather than running off into streets.

✓ Deeper water penetration can help replenish the groundwater in an area. It also encourages worms and other organisms, creating and promoting healthier soil.

✓ When used with a carefully monitored drip system, water harvesting can create a very efficient use of water. Together, drip irrigation and water harvesting create a system that is more easily sustained and maintained over time.

✓ Water harvesting can reduce non-point source water pollution by reducing the volume of water runoff that goes to storm drains.

✓ Harvested rainwater does not require community resources to transport and purify water. It creates a more self-reliant landscape and homeowner.

✓ Harvested water can be stored and used in times of drought.

✓ Rainwater is free.

or capture rainwater as it flows overland, allowing it to infiltrate the soil.

Water harvesting methods can also be incorporated into an existing landscape. Earthworks are fairly straightforward to construct, usually involving no more than a shovel and some labor. They do not involve changing the topography of your surroundings. Types of earthworks include swales, berms (also called watering wells), and boomerangs. Storage possibilities include low-tech rain barrels placed below your home's gutters. The following sections describe some basic earthworks and storage possibilities. The size of these elements will vary depending on your property, its degree of slope, and the amount of rain that falls. However, unless you have guidance from a designer experienced with water harvesting techniques, it's a good idea to start small, see what happens when it rains, and then add more elements as needed. If you miscalculate where the rainwater will flow, or how much of it will accumulate, you can end up with an unplanned reservoir. Many smaller earthworks will usually be more effective in allowing water to soak into the soil than one giant earthwork.

Swales. A swale is a trench dug perpendicular to the slope of the land. Swales can be constructed in just about any size, from a few inches to several feet deep and wide, depending on your site and needs. Swales are best placed in areas of gentle slope, no greater than 30 degrees, with abundant vegetation nearby to make use of the water. It is advantageous to start using swales as high in the landscape as possible to begin the infiltration process and continue installing more swales downslope to keep the overland movement of water at a slow and gentle rate.

Swales don't have to look like ugly trenches but can be formed to look like natural depressions. Each swale should be designed to spill excess water from one of its ends, so the prospect of the system becoming overfilled with runoff and flooding is minimized. You may also use rock to line the top side of the swale and provide additional erosion control. A "riverbed" of rocks in your yard can act as a swale, meandering back and forth so the water has time to soak in. Put plants around it so the roots can benefit from the nearby water source. Since the primary function of a

Earth-Friendly Gardener

Permaculture Instructor Brad Lancaster combines the concepts of swales (fairly level depressions that allow the water to slowly sink in) and mulch pits (mulched depressions that encourage water infiltration) by raising all of his pathways and making sunken planting basins around the pathways. "I use soil from the basins to raise the level of the pathways and then mulch the basins," he says. With raised pathways more rainwater is captured where it can be used—in the planting beds.

Swales are slight depressions where rainwater can accumulate to soak into the soil and irrigate nearby plants. Keep harvested rainwater at least four feet from structures.

swale is to encourage water to soak into the soil, the bottom (water-retaining portion) of the swale may need to be loosened or mulched to assure this infiltration occurs fairly rapidly. No swale should retain water for more than 48 hours to avoid mosquito-borne disease and fungal problems. Ideally, retention times are much less.

Berms/Watering Wells. Some of your trees and shrubs probably already have berms or watering wells, so it would be easy to divert some harvested rainwater to fill them. A berm is a mound of soil encircling a plant (or an area that contains several plants) to hold water in the root zone. Ideally, there should be two mounds of soil, ringing the plant like a doughnut. The inside ring is 4–6 inches away from the plant's stem or trunk and prevents water from standing next to plant tissue for extended periods. The outer ring holds water over the plant's entire root zone so it can slowly penetrate into the soil. Berms should be expanded outward as the plant grows to keep pace with the expanding root zone.

Boomerangs. A boomerang is a berm of soil built in an arc or crescent shape rather than a closed circle. Boomerangs are staggered from the top of a gentle slope to the bottom, slowing both water and soil erosion. They are most effectively constructed on the downhill side of a plant, with water allowed to overflow on one end of the arc. Rainwater accumulates to soak in around the first plant but continues to flow to the next plant down the slope.

Mulch Pits. Mulch pits are holes dug into the ground and then filled

If everyone in the Denver area would consciously work to conserve water, an estimated 83 million gallons could be saved every day. This would equal almost 13 billion gallons per year, enough to fill Mile High Stadium a mile high. That is a lot of water!

—Denver Water Department,
Office of Water Conservation

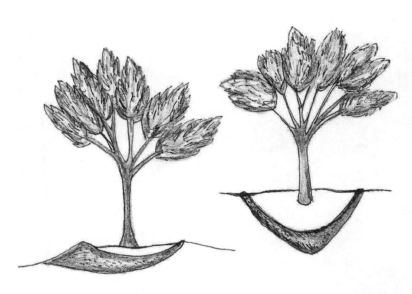

SIDE VIEW

Staggered boomerangs slow rainwater and soil erosion on gentle slopes. Water overflows on the end of the crescent-shaped boomerangs to the next plant.

with mulch. Because the mulch is not as compacted as the soil, the pits act as retention basins for water. They can be filled with any mulch material, such as cardboard, newspaper, grass clippings, leaves, straw, or bark. This material can be covered with granite mulch if you prefer that look, but it is not necessary. Mulch pits work well if dug around young trees when transplanted, before their root systems expand outwards. Mulch pits can be any size and depth, depending on the plants' water requirements and how much water you expect to accumulate. Be careful not to dig into existing root systems.

Storage Containers. In addition to earthworks, a water harvesting system may include cisterns to store water for more controlled distribution. Cisterns can be above- or below-ground, but in the Southwest's hard and rocky soil, digging holes for below-ground storage may be challenging. Storing rainwater is a good option in urban areas where lots are small with little or no slope, making earthworks less useful. Water from rain gutters can be directed into a wide variety of barrels and tanks, such as a large plastic garbage can, several metal barrels connected with a pipe for greater capacity, or a specially designed polyethylene tank that holds thousands of gallons. Avoid buying older used metal tanks because the solder may contain lead. Corrugated metal pipe (CMP), used for drainage under roadways, is starting to be used in harvesting systems, as it is relatively inexpensive given the volume of water it holds. Avoid using rainwater harvested from shingle, tar, or asphalt roofs on edible plants. Metal and tile roofs maintain water quality and the water can be used for all plantings. If properly located, rain barrels should not need pumps or moving parts as the water can be gravity-fed to planting beds.

Earth-Friendly Gardener

Cado Daily, Program Coordinator for the University of Arizona Cooperative Extension's Water Wise Program, installed an eight-foot tall by four-foot wide corrugated metal pipe rainwater storage system at her home. The pipe is set vertically into concrete at the base and a lid covers the top when it is not raining. "When storing water, it's essential to use mosquito screening and cover the water so the larvae can't breed," she states. She also suggests putting a natural biological control into the water called *Bacillus thurengiensis* var. *israelensis*. It is sometimes marketed as a 'mosquito dunk.'

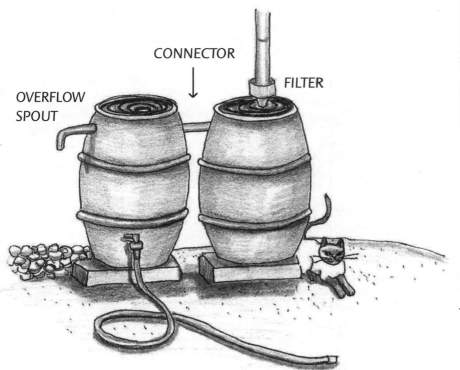

CONNECTOR

OVERFLOW SPOUT

FILTER

Containers can be connected to increase storage capacity from one rain gutter. A filter inhibits debris from getting into the container.

Mosquito Control

If you are going to harvest rainwater to store in containers or build a pond or other water feature in your landscape, it is essential to control for mosquitoes, as they carry the West Nile virus that can be fatal. They can also transmit heartworm to pets. Mosquitoes will lay their eggs in any area that has relatively still water, particularly in shallow water. The water will always be shallow at the edge of a pond, no matter how deep the pond is. Additionally, plants placed around the edges make an excellent habitat for mosquito larvae.

There are three possible mosquito-control measures. The first is to introduce mosquito-eating fish into the pond. Gambusia feed on mosquito larvae at the surface of the water and do not damage plants. The fish grow to about one or two inches in length and resemble guppies. Depending upon the size of the pond, only a few gambusia may be necessary for adequate control. The key is to not allow plants to overgrow an area of the pond, which might prevent the fish from reaching that spot to feed on mosquito larvae.

It is important to realize that gambusia are not native to Arizona or the Southwest. There is concern that they can be introduced into natural water sources and displace native fish. If there is any chance that your pond might be flooded or washed out during heavy rains, with the fish ending up in canals or natural water sources, do not use gambusia. If at some point you dismantle your pond, do not dump fish into canals, lakes, or community water features.

The Arizona Game & Fish Department may offer native fish for mosquito control. A list of their Regional Offices appears in the Resources for Chapter 3. Gambusia fish are available free of charge from Maricopa County Vector Control to any Arizona resident. All states offer some type of biological control for mosquitoes. Check with your local public health or environmental services office for details.

If you do not want to introduce fish into the pond, use mosquito dunks. Many gardeners are familiar with *Bacillus thuringiensis* (Bt), which is a biological control method for caterpillars. Mosquito dunks are made from a specific type of Bt that targets mosquito larvae, *Bacillus thuringiensis* var. *israelensis*.

The final option is to use small doses of chlorine similar to what is used in swimming pools. This will kill the mosquito larvae but does not leave an environment friendly to birds or plants.

Fire and Lightening

The final information for your site assessment is any situation that might encourage the spread of fire. In arid regions, fire and lightning are of concern in both urban and rural areas. Sloped land, in combination with windy conditions, can often contribute to the spread of fire. As a fire travels upslope, it gains in intensity and acceleration. The highest risk occurs when a fire begins in a downslope area and travels upslope, carried and fueled by the wind. In this situation, it would be beneficial to include fire-resistant or low-fuel plants in the downslope area. A well-placed "break" in the landscape, such as a driveway, sitting area, or wide pathway, would also impede the progress of a fire.

In urban situations, the best thing a homeowner can do is assess plant and other materials that would fuel a fire, and move or replace them. High-fuel plant materials, such as dried grasses, weeds, shrubs, and dead plants, located near the house or in the path of prevailing winds should be of utmost concern. It is also important to pay attention to power lines and the possibility of trees growing into or already touching them. Palm trees are particularly hazardous when dead fronds are allowed to accumulate for several years. Palms, like other tall trees or structures, are vulnerable to lightning strikes, which can spread in just moments to nearby homes. Mark any of the above conditions on your site map. *

Chapter 2

Landscape Design

Once your site assessment is complete, you are ready to organize and integrate the information with your aspirations to be more earth friendly. Begin thinking of your landscape as a system. The components of this system work together in mutually beneficial relationships. The three themes of the permaculture framework introduced in Chapter 1 (Care of the Earth, Care of People, Investment in the Future) provide an easy way to identify and organize the components of your landscape system. In completing the following questions, you may find that your responses will overlap. This is a good sign as it indicates areas of connection.

Care of the Earth

Working through the process of site assessment provided many insights into your unique habitat. It gave you the history of the site and a road map to possibilities. Using the information and insights acquired from your assessment, answer the following questions:

❑   What would you like to preserve or restore? This includes preserving existing features in the landscape as well as broader areas of interest such as the preservation and restoration of wildlife habitat or of native culture and traditional ways. Examples of preserving traditions in the Southwest include growing native crops, using adobe bricks, painting walls bright colors, or applying mosaics. (Check with your homeowner's association or community guidelines for possible restrictions.)

❑   Which areas are naturally suited for people? For plants? For animals?

❑   How can I use resources already on-site or readily available in my area? Consider leftover brick, broken concrete, plant starts from other gardeners, knowledge from other people, and products from local artists and retailers.

❑   Will I need to make modifications? Can I make modifications in a way that will enhance the larger ecosystem? For example, using native plants will provide for wildlife and as birds carry the seeds away, they will spread well-adapted plants rather than exotic invasive species from your landscaping.

❑   What natural energies (wind, water, sun) will need to be blocked, diverted, or redirected? Will these modifications help conserve energies? Shade trees save on electric bills and rain barrels save water, and there are possible indirect savings as well. For example, harvesting rainfall saves the energy required to process and transport tap water for landscape purposes.

❑   What situations exist for harvesting rainwater? For recycling graywater into earthworks? Graywater is defined as household wastewater from a clothes washer, bathtub, shower, or bathroom sink. It is used to water landscapes, rather than being sent through a sewage system. Graywater irrigation is described later in the chapter.

❑ Check your human traffic map and identify areas of intense use. These are usually closer to the house and are convenient spots for herb gardens, tool sheds, and plants that need more care and water. This helps save time and energy and reduces human impact in outlying areas. Next, identify areas to be left "wild." Connect them to any identified wildlife corridors in your neighborhood.

❑ Develop a system of connections. Look for multiuse and multi-function opportunities. For example, can you build a swale to collect rainwater that will also help water plants that are a part of a windbreak? Will the trees in the windbreak also help shade a sitting area? Making such mutually beneficial connections is called "stacking functions" and will proportionately increase the sustainability of your design, ensuring that people, plants, and animals all thrive.

❑ What are the surpluses? Do you have an overabundance of any-thing? In permaculture, an overabundance is considered "pollution." Is this overabundance due to a design error? If so, the design should be modified to eliminate the "pollution." For example, planting a shrub that continually needs trimming because the area it is planted in is too small creates green waste and expends human energy. Select another plant for that area or cycle the surplus green waste back into your system as mulch or compost. Using a gas-powered blower to remove leaves from gravel mulch also wastes energy, adds particulates to the air, and creates a pile of surplus leaves that have to be managed in some way. Design the area underneath trees to allow the leaves to drop and create mulch, adding nutrients to the soil to enhance the tree's growth.

Care of People

Make a list of all the possible landscape needs you and your family have. Consider the following questions:

❑ How do you use this space now? How would you in the future? Do you envision a bird sanctuary, play area, or quiet spot for reflection?

❑ How will your lifestyle impact your choices? For example, do you entertain frequently? Do you have young children?

❑ How much available time at home do you have? Do you anticipate this changing in the future? Do you like puttering in the yard or would you prefer a low-maintenance landscape?

❑ What is your activity level? Will you want a volleyball or basket-ball court?

❑ What are your needs for privacy/seclusion, large or small gathering spaces, places for outdoor appreciation/recreation, a place that reflects your personal/cultural expression, or a place to grow edible plants and vegetables?

Earth-Friendly Gardener

Award-winning landscape architect Christy Ten Eyck demonstrates the viability of reusing existing materials at Steele Indian School Park in central Phoenix. There was existing concrete on the site prior to renovation. She chose to reuse it rather than send it to the landfill and pour fresh concrete for the walls. In addition, the concrete is a reminder as to what was there before, the history of the site.

❑   Begin a checklist of ways the system cares for people and conserves human energy, such as shade in a play area, an herb garden close to the kitchen, a site to relax, or placement of the most frequently used or visited items close to the house and pathways.

Investment in the Future

Consider the following ideas to determine the degree to which you are preserving or restoring natural integrity for future generations:

❑   Understand the ecological footprint you are leaving. This is particularly applicable when choosing hardscape materials such as crushed granites, concrete, and pavers. Know where your materials come from and what is involved to process them. How readily can they be reused in the future? In evaluating the environmental cost of a product, consider not only its immediate impact when you use it, but also the environmental cost of producing, packaging, and shipping that product prior to purchase, as well as the cost of disposal after you are finished with it. For example, you may be considering bark chips, decomposed granite, or cement for a pathway in your yard. The accompanying chart presents a method for evaluating the environmental costs. If possible, "live with" the landscape for a while before erecting permanent walls, patios, and similar features.

❑   Use existing resources responsibly. This is the part of the design process where the concepts of reduce, reuse, and recycle need to be seriously considered and implemented. Reduce the need for any materials that quickly degenerate or that over time require a large input of time and money to maintain. Any surplus in the system should be integrated as a resource that enhances. If it can not be integrated into the system, you may want to modify the design. Otherwise, it will become a "pollution" problem for generations to come.

Considerations When Choosing Landscape Materials			
	Wood Chips	**Decomposed Granite**	**Concrete**
Production Method	By-product of lumber or tree-care industry that would otherwise be waste	Mined and crushed	Mined
Packaging	Plastic bags or direct from source without packaging	No packaging	Paper bags or from concrete truck
Pros/Cons While in Use	Allows water to penetrate. No heat accumulation.	Allows water to penetrate. Moderate heat accumulation.	No water penetration. Accumulates heat.
Disposal (if no longer wanted)	Decomposes and releases nutrients and organic matter, benefiting the soil	Must be removed and disposed of	Must be removed and disposed of

❑　Are there available materials that you could recycle instead of buying new? Scout your neighborhood for discarded bricks and broken concrete chunks that can be used to create walkways, patios, and raised beds. Lengths of rebar can be lashed together to make a sturdy trellis. Four wooden shipping pallets make a perfectly sized compost bin. Many stores are ready to give away these pallets because they seldom get reused and it saves them the cost of disposal.

❑　Implement a feedback loop: observe—pay attention—learn what the land teaches you—assess—make needed modifications. You may want to start small and build on your successes.   It is perfectly okay to build your landscape in phases over time. Create your design with the built-in option to change things to meet the changing needs you and your family experience. Modifications are more easily accomplished if sidewalks and patios are set in sand rather than mortar or concrete. Sand setting also creates a surface that is permeable and allows water to penetrate and soak in rather than run into the street.

Sketch Your Ideas on a Bubble Diagram

　A bubble diagram is a rough sketch using lots of circles, or bubbles, showing where you would like to place things in your landscape. An easy way to create a bubble diagram is to overlay your site assessment map with tracing paper. Use a lightweight pencil that can be easily erased and draw simple circles and squares to designate different areas.

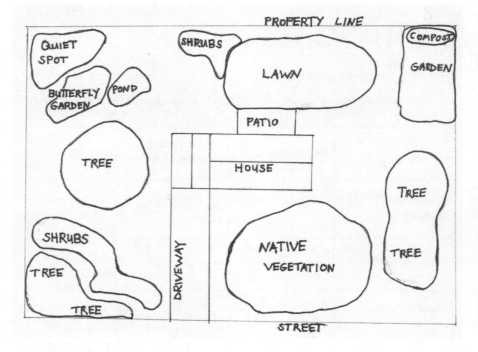

A bubble design is a simple sketch to help you visualize where different elements will fit into your landscape. Use pencil so you can erase and move things around as new ideas occur to you.

Start with your priority items from the list you created in "Care of the People" and work from there. Pay particular attention to how things connect. Find ways of stacking functions, in which plants and other landscape elements have more than one purpose. Be open to the possibilities. Do not expect it all to "fit" together in one sitting. Let yourself have a few hours or even days to sit with an idea. You may need to educate yourself or hire a consultant on a particular area, such as water harvesting or plant selection, before taking action.

Placing Trees and Water Harvesting Earthworks

Trees are vital components of a functioning, earth-friendly system. Mark on your overlay areas needing protection from sun, wind, or cold. Indicate where to place trees for shade, solar arcs, and windbreaks. Be sure the trees you select will have enough room to grow to their mature size. Check on any utility lines in the vertical space the trees will someday occupy.

Review the information in Chapter 1 on water harvesting techniques. As you contemplate where to place water harvesting earthworks, consider the following points. They are reprinted with the permission of Tucson permaculture teacher Brad Lancaster.

❑   Begin with long and thoughtful observation of where and how water flows, not just on your property but in the watershed in your area. What is working, what is not? Build on what works.

❑   Start at the top, the highpoint on your property and work your way down. By starting at the top you can use gravity to direct the water as it naturally travels downhill, and there is less volume and velocity of water.

❑   Start small. Work at a human scale so that you can easily build and repair everything.

❑   Encourage the flow of water to spread and sink. Rather than having water erode the land's surface, encourage it to stick around, flow slowly, and infiltrate into the soil.

❑   Pay special attention to spillways and overflows. Always have an overflow plan for times of extra heavy rains. Use that overflow as a resource.

❑   Maximize vegetative ground cover. Create a living sponge so the harvested water is used to create more resources. The soil will also increase its ability to hold water.

❑   Stack functions in which plants and landscape elements serve more than one function. For example, water harvesting strategies can do more than collect water. Slightly raised berms from swales can act as high and dry paths. Plantings can be selected to encourage wildlife or to provide food for you.

❑   Acknowledge the feedback loop and continue to observe. Continually reassess what you have done and make any needed changes. Modify and learn.

Adding Personal and Cultural Expression

Personal expression may include food growing, flower plantings, artwork, work spaces, and play areas. The landcare history portion of your site assessment should already provide some clues as to the influence of culture in the place you live. Check your overlay. Are your personal needs for expression included? Are there elements that relate to the region's history and culture? This may be a portion of your garden that develops with you over time. Your design should be flexible enough to be easily changed as your personal and family needs change. For example, you may want to reduce the use of crushed rocks in your landscape, especially in the planting beds. The excessive use of crushed rocks can make it difficult to change plantings in the future.

Night Lighting

Treat night lighting in your landscape as an art. When placing the lights, be subtle—less is usually more. Do not place long strings of evenly spaced lights as if hanging lights for a Christmas display. Night lighting should act as an accent to the landscape and help light pathways and steps for safe movement at night.

Set and modify timers according to use and seasonal natural lighting. Most timers will give you the option of two separate run times—one in the evening and one in the early morning.

Buy lights that will last and that you can easily get replacement parts for. If you buy a kit, you do not have to use all of the lights. Keep leftover lights for replacement parts.

Use the appropriate style and number of lights for the area you are lighting. Lights are designed with different functions, such as pathway lights, shrub lights, uplights.

Use motion detector lights for areas where there are security concerns. Twelve-volt lighting should be used primarily as a landscape accent and for safe movement, not as primary security lighting.

Avoid leaving lights on all night. Besides wasting energy, insects (including scorpions) are attracted to the light.

Creating Edge, Outdoor Rooms and Zones

After spending some time observing nature, you may notice there is something unique about the boundary between different habitats. This boundary where different ecologies meet is often referred to as "edge." This unique boundary condition is actually a pattern unto itself. Edges in nature are often very rich places. In addition to the species unique to each adjacent habitat, the edge area often contains unique species of its own. Examples of rich edge areas include the boundary between forest and meadow and the various boundaries between water and dry land.

After observing this richness, you may want to increase edge areas in your design whenever possible. Pathway edges can be increased by having a curving or snaking walkway that meanders like a river. Using a curving pathway can be more aesthetically pleasing and easier to use when trying to follow natural traffic or foot patterns. A hard-surfaced pathway could also be slightly angled to direct water runoff from the pathway into a planting bed. A curved pathway would increase the area of runoff and, therefore, the amount of water that can be directed.

Draw "garden rooms" on your overlay. Examples of outdoor rooms include sitting areas, theme gardens, private spots for contemplation, potting benches, and barbecue and entertainment areas. By creating rooms in your design you will also increase the occurrence of edge. Border this edge with windbreaks, trees and shrubs, different surfaces, a water feature, retaining walls, mounds, and boulders. Include pathways that encourage movement to and from each room.

Larger properties, over one-third an acre, can also use the concept of "zonation" to create a design with more efficiency of movement and to encourage edge. Designing in zones helps economize human energy and preserve and encourage more wild spaces. Zonation can be visualized as a series of concentric circles with Zone 0 (usually the house) at the center. Radiating from the central Zone 0, elements are placed in one of three zones based on the number of times people need to visit the element or the number of times the element requires people to visit. For example, people may pick fresh herbs several times a week or a flower garden may need supplemental watering once a week.

The principles of Xeriscape use a similar concept, labeling the three zones as oasis, transition, and arid, depending on the amount of water the plants use. While there are no hard and fast rules defining each zone, the following examples help illustrate the concept of zones:

Zone 1. Components requiring frequent tending or that are used often should be located closest to the house or near frequently used areas or pathways. Examples include salad gardens or children's play areas.

Zone 2. Components requiring less observation than Zone 1, but still demanding considerable attention. Examples include fruit and citrus trees, greenhouses, vegetable gardens, exotic and ornamental plants.

Zone 3. The "wild" zone includes native plants, wildflower and habitat gardens, and small secluded sitting areas.

Do You Want Turf?

More total acreage is planted in turf grass than any other single crop in the U.S. Many people choose to plant turf in their landscape to reduce erosion and dust, break down air pollutants, decrease the amount of energy needed to cool adjacent buildings, cool the yard, and provide a soft play area for children and pets. A 50 by 50 foot area of turf generates enough oxygen to meet the needs of a family of four.

However, many of those benefits can be achieved without turf. Other, more drought-tolerant groundcovers, shrubs, and trees can provide many of the advantages listed above without the potential problems associated with turf. Lawns consume millions of gallons of water, fertilizer, pesticides, gasoline and oil, as well as countless hours of human energy. The waste products from lawns include huge amounts of grass clippings, most of which end up as green waste in landfills and are often contaminated with excess pesticides and fertilizers. Another waste product of many types of turf is a tremendous amount of pollen to which many people and animals are allergic. An additional waste product is air and noise pollution from the gas-powered mowers and blowers. Inappropriate maintenance of lawns can cause groundwater, air, and soil pollution. It is estimated that 600 million gallons of gas are used annually for lawn care and that homeowners apply 10 times more pesticide per acre of turf than farmers use on an acre of crops.

When designing your landscape, decide if you and your family will actually use and benefit from a grassy area. If you choose to use turf in your landscape, the trick is to find a balance that allows you to capitalize on the benefits of having a lawn while minimizing the associated problems. Determine where you want to install turf, how much you will use, and what type of grass suits your needs.

Location. Choose a spot in the back yard (away from the street) with plenty of sunlight. Most varieties of turf need full sun. If possible, avoid installing grass immediately adjacent to sidewalks, driveways, or walls, as it is hard to position sprinklers without overspray onto these surfaces.

Size. Narrow strips of grass less than eight feet in width do not provide much in the way of recreational use and are difficult to water and mow efficiently. On the other hand, wall-to-wall turf is often wasteful. Strive for an ideally placed and sized practical island of turf.

Type. Different turf grasses are actively growing in the low desert during the warm season and cool season. In warm weather, Bermudagrass is the most common species. It goes dormant and turns brown in cool weather and revives in spring. Select a hybrid variety, planted from stolons or sod. Seeded varieties are higher in pollen and thus more of a problem for allergies. If you choose to have a green lawn year around, Bermudagrass or zoysiagrass can be overseeded with ryegrass for the winter. However, if you allow Bermuda or zoysia to go dormant, your watering and fertilizing chores will be greatly reduced through the winter. (See Earth-Friendly Guide for Watering and Fertilizing Lawns in the Appendix.)

Bermudagrass thrives in the desert because it is a tough grass that takes full sun and is drought tolerant. However, that same toughness allows it to become extremely invasive. It is considered a nuisance weed when it sprouts in a farmer's field or your flower bed. If a lawn does not have a border or if there are wet areas near the turf, Bermudagrass will easily spread with runners, both above- and below-ground. Once established, it is a chore to eliminate. Only plant it where you really want it! Other warm-season possibilities include St. Augustine and buffalograss, although they do not perform well if overseeded. Buffalograss does not require frequent mowing or watering and mixes well with a seeding of wildflowers. Ryegrass is the only species recommended for cool-season planting.

Watering Systems

On average, up to 50 percent of water use is applied to gardens and landscapes in the low desert. In summer, the figure can rise to 60 to 80 percent according to the City of Phoenix Water Conservation Department. A well-designed irrigation system can save water and money if it is regularly maintained and the timer is checked and adjusted monthly. Combined with water harvesting methods, an efficient irrigation system can make plants less vulnerable should restrictions be placed on landscape watering during times of drought. Drip irrigation and graywater systems are two water-saving methods that are described below.

Drip Irrigation

Drip irrigation applies water directly onto the soil at a slow rate, so there is little lost to evaporation from sun and wind. If you have never installed a drip system before, ask for advice from an established retailer that deals exclusively with irrigation. Go to an irrigation supply store and look at the array of parts. It will help you get an idea of how the system fits together. Then sketch another bubble diagram of your site that includes water sources and plant locations. Determine which plants have similar water requirements and can be located in the same area. Putting the design on paper helps you think through all of the elements before you buy the parts and start digging. Spend some time with this because a well-planned watering system will save time and retrofitting later. If you are hiring a landscape company to do it for you, it is still a good idea to draw a diagram (or ask them for one—don't "wing it" on installation day). If you have a basic understanding of your system, it will help you perform simple troubleshooting and maintenance tasks over the long-term, as well as water your plants effectively.

Backflow Prevention Assemblies

These units are required by code for all types of irrigation systems. Their function is to stop contaminated water from being sucked back into your drinking water system. They are typically installed near the water source at least one foot from the wall so there is room to work if repairs are needed. A city permit is required before installation and the Uniform Plumbing Code has specific parameters that must be followed. Thus, it may be easier to hire a licensed contractor to install it for you.

Automatic Timers

All automatic timers (also referred to as controllers) are not the same. Some of the inexpensive controllers available don't have all of the features that allow drip irrigation to be most effective. A good controller should have at least three major functions. First, it should let you set multiple programs, which will accommodate the water needs of different types of plants. For example, lawns need more frequent irrigation than desert trees. Second, it should have the capability to run program durations of at least two hours for shallow-rooted plants, such as groundcovers and perennials, so water soaks through the root system. Run times of four

Play Areas

If you want a play area for children, but don't want to maintain grass:

Develop an intricate system of smooth-surfaced pathways throughout the landscape for children to run and drive play equipment on.

Provide interesting play areas with shade that are incorporated into the landscape. Plan an old-fashioned tree swing or a sandbox adjacent to a mounded area with boulders.

Find a park in your area that provides the space you need. Parks are also a great place for children to socialize. (Let someone else do the mowing!)

hours for shrubs and six or even 12 hours for trees are typically required for water to penetrate through the entire root zone at a slow drip rate. The longer the controller can run, the more flexibility it will provide to effectively water your plants. Look for a timer that allows 6 to 12 hours. Third, the controller should have the option of allowing intervals of 14 days or more between irrigations because plants need less frequent watering in winter than they do in summer. Also, as plants mature, they usually require less frequent irrigation so the length of time between waterings can be extended. Other useful features include a "rain" or "off" setting so you can skip an irrigation without losing the programmed schedule, and a battery back-up to save programs if the power goes out.

To conserve water and grow healthy plants, the timer should be programmed monthly and as plants grow. Take time to learn how to program the controller. Ask the salesperson to explain it and ensure that it is easy for you to operate. If you're hiring a landscape company, tell them what features you want the controller to have before they bid your project. Have them demonstrate it so you can easily program it yourself.

Valves

Valves turn the water supply on and off. When wired to a controller, the valve will open and close on the days and times you have programmed. Many irrigation systems are installed in landscapes with just one or two valves, which is less expensive but may be insufficient if you have varied plant material.

Different types of plants have different water requirements. Desert-adapted plants need less frequent watering than non-adapted species. Trees need deeper watering to wet their root zone than wildflowers or vegetables. Citrus trees need more water than palo verde trees. Newly transplanted plants need more frequent watering than established ones.

When designing your irrigation system, group plants with similar water needs on the same valve. This helps to grow healthy plants and to use water efficiently. For example, if one valve is watering both citrus trees and desert shrubs, it would be difficult to program it so that both types of plants received the optimum water. If the citrus is watered correctly, the desert shrubs are probably being watered too frequently with more water than they need; if the desert shrubs are watered correctly, the citrus is probably being underwatered. Plants that are not overwatered or underwatered are healthier, less susceptible to pests and diseases, and less likely to need costly replacement. If you have varied plant material or may be changing your landscape over time, install sufficient valves or ask the landscape maintenance company to do so. This will cost more initially, but saves time and money later.

Drip Emitters

There are several methods for applying drip irrigation. Drip emitters are small plastic devices about the size of a thumbnail. They regulate the flow of water, typically allowing 1, 2, or 4 gallons of water per hour. Some adjustable emitters range from 0 to 10 gallons per hour. Emitters are usually plugged into the end of thin polyethylene tubing, called "spa-

Earth-Friendly Gardener

Donna DiFrancesco, City of Mesa Water Conservation Specialist is co-author of *Desert Landscaping for Beginners* and *Landscape Watering by the Numbers*. She regularly counsels homeowners on effective irrigation techniques. "It is generally a good idea to buy a controller that will handle more valves, sometimes called stations, than you need," she suggests. "If you know you need one valve for shrubs, one for trees, and two valves for grass, you need a controller that handles four valves. Buy a five- or six-valve capacity controller, just in case you need to add one in the future, or decide to change your landscape."

ghetti tubing," which in turn is connected to thicker poly tubing that is buried below the soil surface. "In-line" emitters are another style and are contained within the tubing itself. "Laser tubing" and "soaker hoses" don't have individual emitters, but their purpose is also to deliver water slowly. Laser tubing has pinprick-sized holes uniformly spaced by a laser (thus the name) every six inches or so along the tubing. Soaker hose "weeps" water along its entire length.

Placing Drip Irrigation Around Plants

The placement of drip irrigation is important to properly water plants and to conserve water. Plants that will remain small (1-3 feet in diameter) such as groundcovers and perennials may require only one emitter, but larger plants should have emitters spaced evenly around the perimeter to encourage balanced root growth. As a tree or shrub grows, it is essential to move whatever type of drip you are using outwards to keep pace with the expanding root zone. Have you ever seen emitters tightly grouped next to the thick trunk of a mature tree? They were installed when the tree was a sapling and nobody bothered to move them as the tree grew. Any water these emitters might still be putting out is wasted unless there are other small plants growing at the base, as the tree's "feeder" roots have long since outgrown the area. The tree's feeder roots, which take up water and nutrients, are constantly expanding outward, past its canopy edge or dripline (where rainfall would drip off the foliage to the ground). Water deposited near the trunk of a mature tree will not reach these feeder roots.

It may also be necessary to add more emitters as plants grow to ensure enough water is applied. Assume you start with three two-gallon emitters around a young tree. Running the system for one hour provides 6 gallons of water, which won't be sufficient to maintain the tree as it grows.

A potential problem with drip irrigation is to let it run frequently for short periods of time, such as daily for 15 minutes. This practice provides insufficient water for most plants. It also allows salts to accumulate in the root zone, which is unhealthy for the plant. With each irrigation, water should be applied to soak deeply enough to leach salts beyond the root zone. (Chapter 4 provides more information on how deep to water.) That is why it is important to choose a timer that allows lengthy run-times.

Graywater Irrigation

Graywater is household wastewater originating from a clothes washer, bathtub, shower, or bathroom sink. It can not originate from a kitchen sink, dishwasher, or toilet because of the possibility of contaminants or the spread of disease. If allowed by your state and local regulations, graywater may be diverted from a standard wastewater disposal system and used to irrigate your landscape.

Proponents of graywater reuse cite the vast amount of clean drinking water that could be saved. On the other hand, there have been concerns about the possible spread of disease, contamination of existing water supplies, and the long-term effects on plants and soil if graywater is used. That is why it is essential to follow guidelines for graywater systems as established by your state. The State of Arizona changed its regulations regarding graywater in 2001. It is no longer necessary to submit design plans or water samples to the Arizona Department of Environmental Quality or to apply for an actual permit. However, residents must meet all of the guidelines on this page for a Reclaimed Water Type 1 General Permit and all 13 of the "Best Management Practices" (BMPs) as described by the State. Local governments may have more restrictive policies, so check with your city or county before proceeding.

Type 1 General Permit Best Management Practices (BMPS) for Graywater Use in Arizona

1. First and foremost, avoid human contact with graywater.

2. You may use graywater for household gardening, composting, and lawn and landscape irrigation, but it should not run off your own property.

3. Do not surface irrigate any plants that produce food, except citrus and nut trees.

4. Use only flood or drip irrigation to water lawns and landscaping. Spraying graywater is prohibited.

5. When determining the location for your graywater irrigation, remember that it cannot be in a wash or drainage way.

6. Graywater may only be used in locations where groundwater is at least five feet below the surface.

7. Label pipes carrying graywater under pressure if confusion between graywater and drinking water pipes is possible.

8. Cover, seal and secure storage tanks to restrict access by small rodents and to control disease-carrying insects (including mosquitoes).

9. Hazardous chemicals, such as antifreeze, mothballs, and solvents can not be in graywater. Do not include wash water from greasy or oily rags in your graywater.

10. Graywater from washing diapers or other infectious garments must be discharged to a residential sewer or other wastewater facility, or it can be disinfected prior to use.

11. Surface accumulation of graywater must be kept to a minimum.

12. Should a backup occur, graywater must be disposed into your normal wastewater drain system. To avoid such a backup, consider using a filtration system to reduce plugging and extend the system's lifetime.

13. If you have a septic or other on-site wastewater disposal system, graywater use does not change that system's design requirements.

Reprinted from "Using Graywater at Home," Arizona Department of Environmental Quality Publication C 01-06.

Reclaimed Water Type 1 General Permit Guidelines for the State of Arizona

✓ This general permit is for residential use only.

✓ Graywater must be used on the site where it is generated.

✓ There must be no access by the public.

✓ Graywater can be used only for irrigation (no dust control or cooling).

✓ Graywater can not be sprayed.

✓ Less than 400 gallons per day can be used.

Other Factors to Consider Before Using Graywater

Graywater systems can be simple or elaborate, inexpensive or costly. Each household has unique needs with individual plumbing systems, water-use patterns, soil types, landscapes, and budgets. It is impossible to design a ready-made system that works for all situations. Like any household improvement or building project, it is a good idea to do plenty of research and consult a variety of experts before proceeding. Any plumbing work requires a permit and inspection and must comply with the Uniform Plumbing Code. Contact your city building department for more information. If following the Permit Guidelines and BMPs on the previous page is feasible for you, consider the following points to help you decide if graywater makes sense for your household. If so, use the listings in the Resources to obtain more specific design ideas.

❑ Don't use graywater on your landscape if you have a water softening system. The graywater will have large concentrations of salts which are harmful to plants.

❑ Know your soil type. Will graywater readily drain through it and not pool on the surface? Sandy soils drain more readily than clay soils. If you're not sure, test areas of your landscape with a slow-running hose to see how quickly water soaks in.

❑ Determine how much graywater your household will potentially generate using the following formula: Number of family members x 35 gallons per day. Can your proposed graywater system handle that? Do you have enough plants and landscape area to accommodate the water? Even though you are using graywater, it is still essential to follow efficient watering guidelines.

❑ Graywater shouldn't be dispensed next to buildings as it can damage the foundation over time. Do you have at least four feet between the building and graywater outlets?

❑ What plants do you want to water and where are they in relation to the proposed graywater outlets? Are they on an uphill slope? If so, how will the water reach them? It is generally recommended to apply graywater to landscape plants and fruit or nut trees, but avoid using it on other food plants.

❑ Will the cost of the system (including energy costs to manufacture, transport, and install the parts) repay itself in water savings? What is the projected lifespan of the system? Will many components need to be replaced frequently? If you sell your home, will the new owners find the system easy to use and maintain?

❑ Retrofitting an existing home will be more expensive than installing a system during initial house construction. Plumbing drainage pipes must be readily accessible. If laundry facilities are in the garage or bathrooms next to an outside wall, it is more feasible to install a graywater system than if they are located in the home's interior.

**? How Much Graywater ?
Do You Generate**

The average person produces 35 gallons of graywater per day.

What About Soap Residues in Graywater?

There has been little research evaluating the effects of graywater containing consumer products, such as laundry detergent or shampoo, on the plants, soil, or water supply. One such study was conducted by César Mazier, as Director of Horticulture at the Desert Botanical Garden in Phoenix. He used graywater from Desert House to determine its effects on the growth of desert plants. (Desert House is an on-going project that monitors actual water and energy use by its occupants. It is located on the grounds of the Desert Botanical Garden.) He tested for differences between the use of graywater and city water in such areas as plant tissue nutrient levels, soil conditions, and water salinity. Although on some measures statistically significant differences were found, the two-year study concluded that overall growth was not significantly different for plants watered with graywater or city water. Water was also sampled for the presence of fecal coliforms, with *E. coli* as the indicator. This bacteria was present in one of the graywater samplings. This result emphasizes the need to use extreme care with graywater systems, following the permit guidelines and BMPs to reduce the likelihood of spreading or contracting water-borne illnesses.

Excessive amounts of sodium, chlorine, or boron, which are often found in laundry products, can kill plants. Since every household uses different types of cleaners in variable quantities, it is difficult to predict what effects might occur. Monitor your plants regularly for changes in foliage appearance such as yellowing, brown leaf edges, or dieback, which might indicate a problem from the graywater. It is a good idea to occasionally irrigate deeply with your regular water source to help leach accumulated salts below the root zone.

Creating a Wildfire-Resistant Landscape

Drought conditions seem to be the norm throughout the arid Southwest, making both water conservation and fire prevention a priority for residents. In recent years, devastating wildfires have swept across hundreds of thousands of forest, grassland, and desert acres throughout the region, destroying hundreds of homes. Even so, firefighting crews worked relentlessly to save thousands more. They were most successful saving structures that had "defensible space."

Defensible space is created by reducing the amount of flammable material in the area surrounding the building. By reducing the fuel load, you reduce the ability of the fire to approach and consume the building. *If your home is in an area at-risk for wildfires, it is imperative to create defensible space before wildfires occur.* Homes with defensible space *and* a non-flammable roof have an even greater likelihood of survival.

Components of Fire

There are three factors influencing how a fire starts and how fast it spreads: fuel, weather, and topography.

Fuel. Dead plant material (twigs, dried leaves, needles, seed pods, pine cones, dried grasses, dead trees and branches) and living plant material are the main sources of fuel, but homes and other structures will add to available fuel if they are in the path of a wildfire. Also consider stacks of firewood, wooden fences, gasoline or other flammables stored in sheds and garages, and even junk piles. Pay attention to what sources of fuel neighbors may have.

Weather. Fires start more easily and burn more rapidly during hot, dry, and windy weather.

Topography. As a fire travels upslope, it gains in intensity and acceleration. The steeper the slope, the faster the fire travels. South and southwest slopes are hotter and drier than northern slopes and therefore usually experience more fires.

Four Steps to Designing Defensible Space

Defensible space does not have to equal large stretches of bare soil devoid of plants. The type and quantity of plant material and how it is spaced and maintained are crucial factors in reducing a fire's intensity and how fast it spreads. You can't change the weather or the lay of the land, but you can reduce the amount of fuel available by choosing plants that are more fire resistant than others, placing them far enough apart, and caring for them regularly.

1. Determine the size of your defensible space.

As a guideline, the area between the house and a 30-foot perimeter surrounding it should be managed as defensible space. Actual distance will vary depending on the slope of the land, the type of native vegetation that surrounds it, and the characteristics of your lot. The steeper the slope and the more flammable the plant material, the greater the defensible space should be. If your home is on a 40 percent slope and surrounded by heavy plant material during drought conditions, 200 feet might be required as defensible space. Desert plants that are highly flammable, such as creosote and chaparral sage, can be extremely volatile, allowing fire to spread even more quickly than in a pine forest. If you are surrounded by this type of vegetation, consider doubling the size of your defensible space.

On small urban lots, there may not be enough property to create 30 feet of defensible space surrounding buildings. It is still important to assess the situation and move or replace plants and materials that would create fuel. Start by determining the direction of the prevailing wind. If a fire starts nearby, it will probably spread in the direction of the prevailing wind. As stated in Chapter 1, prevailing winds in the Southwest usually come from the southwest. What is in the southwest corner of your property? What materials does your neighbor's yard have adjacent to it? Are there stacks of firewood, leftover building supplies, or lots of pine needles that seldom get raked? In such a situation, your defensible space may be concentrated in that corner of your property.

2. Remove any existing dead vegetation, such as branches or dried-out plant material, within the defensible space.

Defensible Space Should Be:

Lean: Very little flammable plant material.

Clean: No dead plant material accumulating on the ground or left on plants.

Green: Healthy, low-fuel plants during the height of the fire season.

Mow or cut down dried grasses and wildflowers. If possible, wait until wildflowers go to seed, so plants can self-sow for the following year. Reduce the depth of pine needles on the ground to two inches. Do not remove all needles, which will create soil erosion problems. As an alternative, use hardscape elements (stepping stones, decorative rock, granite mulches) to lay out paths that create "breaks," slowing a fire's spread across your landscape.

3. Eliminate potential "fuel ladders."

A fuel ladder exists when plants of varying heights are located near each other, encouraging the fire to jump from one "rung" to the next. For example, a layer of dried pine needles on the ground can ignite a serviceberry shrub, and then move to the branches of a pine tree. When the fire reaches the canopies of these tall pine trees, burning stems and branches can be "thrown" forward through the forest, in a condition called "spotting." If you live in timberland areas, remove branches on pine trees in your defensible space to a height of 10 feet above the ground to reduce the potential of fuel ladders.

Fuel ladders allow fire to easily spread from low-growing plants into nearby trees. Eliminate fuel ladders in your defensible space.

Native low desert does not have quite the same problem of fuel ladders as does forest land, because the desert trees are not as tall and much of the vegetation is more widely spaced. Even so, non-native grasses and other small plants that flourish after rainy periods, and then dry out, create a ready source of fuel that allows fire to spread quickly across the desert, especially when fanned by strong winds. Remove this type of dried plant material in your landscape to reduce the available fuel for a fire.

In high-desert grassland areas, fires can travel extremely fast when driven by a strong wind through dried plant material. Mow around homes and outbuildings frequently to keep the grass cover short.

4. Create space between individual plants or small groups of plants within your defensible space.

The following points are more applicable if you live in a house surrounded by native vegetation, as opposed to an urban environment.

❑ Do not plant within three to five feet of any structure.

❑ Plants near structures should be low-growing and widely spaced. Do not use dense masses of plants, which provide a continuous source of fuel.

❑ If possible, do not have trees within 15 feet of the house. If you must keep an existing tree, expand the size of the defensible space around it. Remove branches up to 10 feet above the ground. Do not allow the tree to touch the home or other trees.

❑ Allow at least 10 feet between the edges of mature tree canopies and large shrubs. This is measured between each plant's widest-reaching branch (not between trunks). For example, if planting trees that will have a 30-foot canopy at maturity, such as mesquite, plant them 40 feet apart (15-foot allowance from each tree, plus 10 feet between them). If you live on a slope, where fire will travel more rapidly, allow more space between each tree.

❑ Place firewood and compost bins at least 30 feet from the home, uphill if possible. If they catch fire, flames are more likely to continue uphill, away from the house.

Begin to Create Your Landscape Design

By referencing the site assessment and bubble diagram overlays you have created, you should have enough information to start filling in the details of your design. Your site assessment overlays provide you with a working reference specific to your yard, your bioregion, and your particular needs. If you hire a professional, look for someone who appreciates and honors that work. If you decide to complete the design on your own, you may want to enlist a friend to whom you can present your design. This person does not have to know anything about gardening or landscaping. By verbally presenting your design to someone else, you will quickly discover the areas that are not connecting and may need more thought. This verbal presentation exercise will also bring out ideas and stimulate more practical and creative connections to enhance your overall design. The next chapter covers selecting plants for your landscape. ✳

Chapter 3

Plant Selection

Walking up and down nursery aisles, it is easy to be swept away the moment your eyes alight on a leafy shrub filled with hot pink blossoms. Impressed with its beauty, you quickly load it onto the cart without considering if it is really the best plant for all of your needs. Like candy bars at the grocery store check-out lane, it is an impulse buy, often regretted! It may seem faster to fill the cart with whatever plants strike your fancy, but a little energy spent on appropriate plant selection will save you time and money in the long run. Although there are hundreds of plants to consider, the following points will help you narrow the choices and decide which will work best in your landscape:

- ❑ Select the right plant for the right place.
- ❑ Choose drought-tolerant native and desert-adapted plants.
- ❑ Plan for the plant's mature size.
- ❑ Use multipurpose plants.

Select the Right Plant for the Right Place

Identify the key characteristics of your planting site and then select a plant that will thrive there. What do you have to offer the plant? Consider climate, soil type, water needs, sunlight, and amount of space. Choosing plants that are well suited for your landscape's characteristics and that fulfill your specific needs and desires as determined from the first two chapters of this book will save considerable time, money, and frustration. Smart plant choices result in healthier plants, fewer routine maintenance chores, infrequent pest and disease problems, and ultimately, fewer dead plants requiring replacement.

Choose Drought-Tolerant Native and Desert-Adapted Plants

Native plants form the backbone of any earth-friendly landscape, although using natives doesn't mean that exotic plants are forbidden. However, concentrating on native and other well-adapted plants from growing regions similar to your own offers many advantages and provides extra time for maintaining non-native plants that may be especially appealing to you.

Native plants have adapted over hundreds and perhaps thousands of years to a region's specific growing conditions. Much of the Southwest experiences scant rainfall, scorching summer sun, drastic temperature fluctuations, and alkaline soil containing very little organic matter. Desert plants have evolved to thrive in these surroundings. Once established, they don't require time and money spent on supplemental watering and fertilizing. Planting natives is a low-maintenance method to save water and maintain water quality as will be explained further.

Other regions around the country have vastly different growing conditions than the desert. For example, the Pacific Northwest has somewhat acidic soil rich in organic matter, plentiful rainfall, and moderate temperatures. Obviously, plants native to the Southwest would struggle in the Northwest, and plants native to the Northwest would struggle in the desert. There is little value in forcing plants from a dramatically different region to grow in your conditions. Trying to recreate specific characteristics, such as lowering an alkaline soil pH to an acidic pH, is difficult, expensive, and the results are short term at best. Struggling, stressed plants are more likely to be attacked by pests and diseases. Because native plants have developed resistance to local pest problems, they require little or no intervention with pesticides.

Another valuable reason for choosing native plants is that native wildlife can use them for food, shelter, and nesting sites. Planting natives helps to re-establish at least small sections of habitat lost to development. Migratory bird patterns can continue as they have for hundreds of years, as your landscape provides them with a refueling stop.

Plan for the Plant's Mature Size

This concept is often overlooked, but it's an essential component of selecting plants for a well-planned landscape. It may be difficult to imagine those leafless sticks in one-gallon containers growing to be sweeping shrubs or towering trees, although they quickly do! Before purchase, determine the mature size of all plants and ensure that they will fit in the space you have allotted. Will a tree have room to

stretch to its full height without bumping into utility wires, the ever-expanding canopies of nearby trees, or your neighbor's rooftop? Will a shrub or agave be able to spread to its full width and maintain its beautiful natural branching pattern without stabbing an unsuspecting passerby?

Unfortunately, when a plant grows too tall or wide for its space, it usually gets kept in bounds by regular pruning. This trimming may serve a purpose but has two negative effects: it creates green waste and pruning wounds.

Green Waste

Green waste is composed of trimmings from trees and shrubs, grass clippings, and other landscape leftovers. Approximately 30–50 percent of the material sent to landfills is green waste. Frequently pruning a plant because it is too tall or wide for its space contributes to the overload placed on our landfill systems. Contrary to popular belief, green waste does not rapidly decay in the landfills. Both oxygen and water are required for decomposition to readily take place. All refuse is tightly compacted with heavy machinery, which forces out available oxygen, and there is scant rainfall or soil moisture in the Southwest. Archaeology professor and "garbologist" William Rathje of the University of Arizona and his students have studied landfill waste since the 1970s, using a bucket

Allow space for plants to grow to their mature size without crowding or unnecessary pruning to keep them away from walkways.

augur to dig up samples in numerous sites. The results show that only about half of the green waste and food items decompose. Finding fully readable newspapers is commonplace, which allows dating other materials that are still intact, including 15-year-old hot dogs! A more earth-friendly solution to overflowing landfills is to reduce the amount of green waste you generate and recycle the rest back into the landscape as compost or mulch.

Pruning Wounds

Pruning creates open wounds that allow easy access for pests and diseases. Pruning stresses plants and can reduce their lifespan. If you or your landscapers are constantly trimming and shearing trees and shrubs just to keep them a manageable size, it is likely that you have the wrong plant in the wrong place. It is also likely that you are "forcing" the plant into a shape that is unnatural for its genetic make-up. In this case, it may be better to remove it and replace it with a plant that is more suited for that location. Most native plants have branching patterns that are far more attractive if you allow them to assume their natural shape.

Use Multipurpose Plants

Select plants that fulfill more than one purpose, thus providing more benefits for the same investment, whether measured by water, fertilizer, or time, money, and energy saved. Choose plants that provide ornamental interest throughout the year, such as flowers, foliage color, seed pods, and bark texture. For example, a palo verde tree gives fabulous spring bloom and in summer provides birds with tasty seed pods. During summer, the tree provides valuable shade; because it is deciduous, the leaves will drop in winter and the sun's rays can shine through to warm your home. This saves on energy bills year around. As a native tree, the palo verde will thrive with limited water and fertilizer, helping to conserve resources.

The National Wildlife Federation sponsors a Backyard Habitat certification program and provides information to create wildlife habitats at homes, schools, communities, and workplaces. They have certified over 25,000 habitats. Contact them at: Backyard Habitat Program, 11100 Wildlife Center Dr., Reston, VA 20190-5362, 800-822-9919, www.nwf.org.

There are many examples of multipurpose plants. A citrus tree requires regular water and fertilizer, but the tree also provides shade, intoxicating fragrance when in bloom, and fresh fruit. Because it has a dense canopy, it can serve as a privacy screen. Citrus attracts beautiful giant black and yellow swallowtail butterflies, who lay their eggs on the foliage. When they hatch, the caterpillars consume leaves, but won't harm an otherwise healthy and established tree. A Mexican tarragon (*Tagetes lucida*) shrub provides flowers, fragrance, and leaves that can be used in cooking. The following sections on wildlife habitats, edible landscaping, low-allergen gardens, and fire-resistant landscapes provide ideas for choosing plants that are multifunctional.

Selecting Plants for Wildlife Habitats

One of the special joys of gardening is the opportunity to view small creatures—birds, butterflies, insects, lizards, toads, and other wildlife—up close and personal as they go about their daily activities. Hummingbirds hover just an arm's length away, inserting their narrow beaks into tubular-shaped penstemon blossoms. Lizards warm themselves in the sun, ready to scurry for protection under vine-covered walls. Butterflies alight nearby, sipping from nectar-rich flowers.

Wouldn't it be relaxing to enjoy this infinite variety of nature daily by simply looking out the kitchen window or sitting on the patio with a glass of lemonade? Creating a wildlife habitat in your yard is not difficult or expensive, and it will encourage a multitude of visitors. It is especially important to provide habitat in heavily populated urban areas where most natural spaces have been eliminated by development. Creating a wildlife habitat with your children is an entertaining family activity encouraging them to connect with nature and become stewards of a healthy ecosystem.

The Four Essentials: Water, Food, Shelter, and Nesting Sites

The sound of water will attract birds and other wildlife to your garden.

Wild creatures require the same basic elements that humans need to exist—water, food, shelter from predators and weather, and a safe place to raise offspring. According to the National Wildlife Federation's Backyard Habitat Program, the most effective way to attract native wildlife species is to landscape with native plants. Many plants and animals have evolved an intricate, precisely timed system to ensure each other's survival. It makes sense that wildlife will seek out the same plants they have relied on over hundreds of years. Creating a complete habitat also gives you and your children the opportunity to observe the fascinating life cycle of a species, including courting behavior, nest building, and rearing young.

Water. Water for drinking and bathing is an essential component of any habitat. Water sources can be as simple as a slight depression in a large rock, mimicking where rain might collect in the wild, or as elaborate as a small waterfall tumbling into a backyard pond. What is most important is that the water remains clean to prevent the spread of disease. Flowing or dripping water stays fresh longer. If you use standing water sources, such as birdbaths, scrub them every few days with a 10 percent bleach solution (9 parts water and 1 part bleach) and let them dry in the sun. This is crucial during warm weather, both to prevent the spread of disease and the breeding of mosquitos. (See Chapter 1 for mosquito control methods.)

Most birds can access water in birdbaths, but other types of wildlife need to drink at ground level. Birds are attracted to the sound of water, and even an exceedingly slow drip from a faucet or irrigation system into a shallow saucer will attract wildlife. If small animals could possibly fall into a deeper water source, provide a way for them to climb out, such as stepping stones or a slanted piece of wood. If there are predators around, especially household pets, situate the water in the open where there is no cover for them to lie in wait and pounce upon unsuspecting wildlife.

Food, Shelter, and Nesting Sites. Native plants sustain wildlife populations by providing food, shelter, and nesting sites throughout the year. They support the tiniest insects at the bottom of the food chain up to the large mammals at the top. The bonus for gardeners is twofold: native plants usually require less water and fertilizer than exotic species and they are less susceptible to insect and disease problems. Gardeners save precious water resources, time, and money while eliminating the use of synthetic pesticides. Most pesticides are indiscriminate, killing beneficial insects as well as pests. Refraining from pesticide use is a crucial component to creating a wildlife habitat. Insects are an important food source for many birds and lizards. If your plants are healthy, they can withstand small numbers of pests and the wildlife attracted to your landscape will consume the insects.

The greater variety of plants, the more likely diverse creatures will come to your garden. In addition, think vertically as well as horizontally when designing your habitat. Different species live and forage at different levels. When is the last time you saw quail in the tree tops or hawks scurrying on the ground? The more "safety zones" at varying levels that a landscape provides, the more potential habitats it creates. Copy nature's design and plant varying heights of trees, large and small shrubs, perennial flowers, and groundcovers. Stagger them in drifts and naturalistic groupings rather than straight lines. Use rock piles, brush piles, and hollow logs (if fire hazard is not a consideration) to provide shelter and add to your habitat's diversity.

As plants grow, allow them to assume their natural flowing shapes instead of pruning them into cubes, balls, and other tortured geometric shapes. Branches that drape the ground provide quick cover and safety from predators: it is difficult to hide under a plant pruned into a lollipop shape. Constantly pruning plants eliminates flowers and seeds, both valuable food sources. Transplant more groundcovers in place of gravel mulches, in which both seeds and insects sink below the reach of birds. If your landscape is already quite full, incorporate plants that flower or provide seeds during a season when the existing plants do not.

The Plant List in the Appendix lists plants that will attract wildlife. Check the Resource section for native plant and wildlife organizations. They can also provide information on appropriate plants to attract native creatures in your area.

Plant Guilds

In nature, many species of plants and animals thrive together by providing direct or indirect assistance to each other. In our landscapes, we can design similar mutually beneficial groupings, called "plant guilds." Plants work together to increase humidity, reduce evaporation rates, add organic matter to the soil, and provide wind and sun protection. Plant guilds are also highly beneficial for native wildlife, providing food, protection, and places to rear young. Completing the loop, animal species assist the plants by providing insect control, pollination, seed dispersal, and nutrients. When designing a guild, think about grouping plants in a "multistory" effect, in which three tiers of plants are used—groundcovers, shrubs, and trees. This mirrors nature and is also aesthetically pleasing. These plant groupings help promote a sustainable landscape that requires less intervention on your part. The ironwood tree illustration on the next page is an excellent example of a guild.

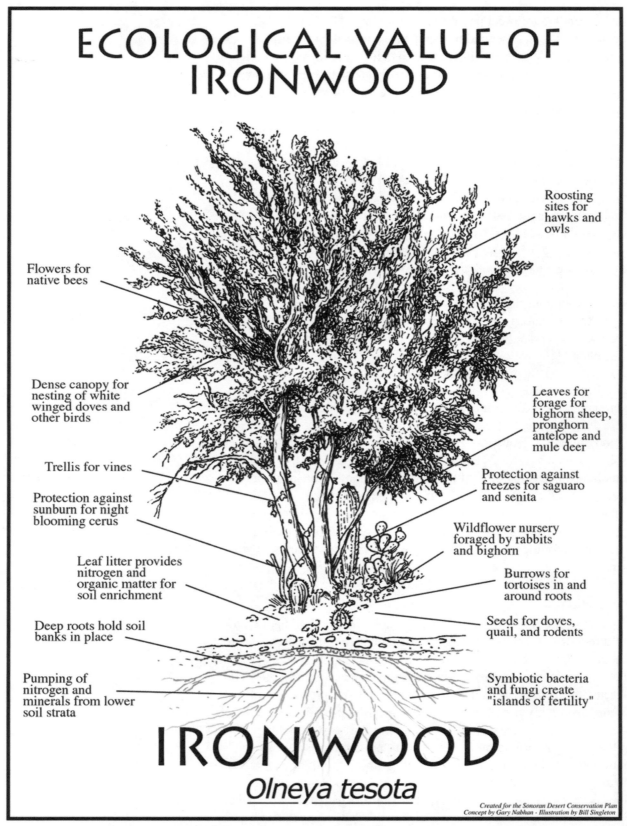

ECOLOGICAL VALUE OF IRONWOOD

Roosting sites for hawks and owls

Flowers for native bees

Dense canopy for nesting of white winged doves and other birds

Leaves for forage for bighorn sheep, pronghorn antelope and mule deer

Trellis for vines

Protection against freezes for saguaro and senita

Protection against sunburn for night blooming cerus

Wildflower nursery foraged by rabbits and bighorn

Leaf litter provides nitrogen and organic matter for soil enrichment

Burrows for tortoises in and around roots

Deep roots hold soil banks in place

Seeds for doves, quail, and rodents

Pumping of nitrogen and minerals from lower soil strata

Symbiotic bacteria and fungi create "islands of fertility"

IRONWOOD
Olneya tesota

Created for the Sonoran Desert Conservation Plan
Concept by Gary Nabhan - Illustration by Bill Singleton

The native ironwood tree is an example of a multipurpose plant that provides food and habitat for native wildlife as well as shade, color, and beauty for humans. This setting is an example of a plant guild, in which plants and animals co-exist in mutually beneficial relationships. (Illustration originated for the Sonoran Desert Conservation Plan and reprinted by permission of the artist.)

Attracting Birds

Bird watching has long been a popular activity in our country. At first glance, birdfeeders seem to be a quick and easy method to attract birds. Although it is pleasing to view a flock around a feeder, it is not as beneficial to the birds over the long term as creating a habitat that contains the four essentials of water, food, shelter, and nesting sites.

If you choose to put out birdseed, feeders should be cleaned and disinfected every three to seven days, as well as moved to new locations to prevent the build-up of droppings and the spread of disease. Many birds feeding in one area increase the likelihood of deadly disease spreading among the flock or across species. Supplying birdseed often attracts feral pigeons, which are generally considered nuisance birds. Either pigeons or their droppings are capable of transmitting at least 40 diseases to humans and animals. Use elevated feeders that do not spill onto the ground to discourage pigeons.

Birds eat insects, seeds, fruits, and/or nectar, so the more variety in your plant offerings, the greater assortment of birds popping by for lunch. Some birds are selective about what they eat; others take the buffet approach. "At some point in their lives, almost all birds consume insects," states Joe Yarchin, Regional Urban Wildlife Specialist with the Arizona Game & Fish Department. "Parents feed their babies a diet of insects, which are easier to digest than seeds or fruit." Refrain from spraying pesticides on your plants and let birds perform pest-elimination chores.

Seed eaters such as quail, finches, sparrows, and doves can forage under palo verde, ironwood, and mesquite trees, as well as numerous native shrubs, including catclaw (*Acacia greggii*, not to be confused with the catclaw vine), desert hackberry, fairy duster, four-wing saltbush, hopbush, brittlebush, and the aptly named quailbush. A few flowers that provide for seed eaters are desert marigold, lupine, sunflower, poppy, and tufted evening primrose.

Many desert hikers have seen a nest constructed by a cactus wren, Arizona's state bird, sandwiched among the protective arms of a cholla cactus. Ironwood trees are another favorite nesting site and the wrens use soft flower heads from fairy dusters to line their nests.

Desert plants provide a feast for hummingbirds, who insert their beaks into tubular shaped flowers to obtain nectar. They can dart amongst penstemon, aloe, justicia, salvia, desert willow, ocotillo, and hummingbird trumpet.

Many bird species are fruit and berry eaters and they will seek out Mexican elderberry, a tree that can reach 30 feet in height. Other choices include desert hackberry, barberry, gray thorn, wolfberry, and many species of prickly pear cacti with their deep red fruits. The Sonoran Desert's signature plant, the saguaro, also provides an important food source in June and July when its juicy red fruits are in season. Native plants also provide for migratory birds that seem to come through at opportune times to take advantage of the desert bounty. For example, hooded orioles are attracted to blooms on agaves and sweet acacia trees, and they also eat the insects attracted to the blooms. Phainopepla feed on desert mistletoe berries, providing a good reason to keep a "wild" area on larger properties.

Earth-Friendly Gardener

Cathy Rymer, co-author of *Desert Landscaping for Beginners,* created a wildlife habitat in her backyard using native plants. The ironwood tree is the site of three verdin nests. "This is the only tree in my yard that has bird nests," reports Cathy. "I'm sure one of the features that makes this tree so attractive to birds are the thorns. My cats have an aversion to thorns."

Butterfly Gardens

The most effective way to attract these delightful winged insects is to provide not only nectar sources for the adult butterfly but food plants for butterfly larvae—or caterpillars. The caterpillars are selective and usually feed on just one or two types of plants, called "host plants." If you grow these, it is likely that your garden will become a favored site for butterflies seeking a place to deposit eggs.

Butterflies evolve through four stages: egg, larval, pupal, and adult. The life cycle begins with a butterfly laying an egg on its favored host plant. The egg hatches into a caterpillar, which eats the food source for two to four weeks until it is full grown. It then seeks a safe place to pupate, surrounding itself with a protective casing called a cocoon. In one of nature's most magical events, the caterpillar transforms into an adult butterfly and emerges from the cocoon.

The caterpillars may seem to be voraciously consuming an entire plant, but if the plant is healthy and has an established root system, it should recover. Because caterpillars are specific about what they eat, they won't decimate an entire garden. Resist the urge to control them.

Adult butterflies are not as fussy about their food and will sip sugary nectar from a wide variety of sources. They visit different flowers in the wild than in developed areas. Some commonly grown flowering plants that butterflies frequent include lantana, verbena, salvia, mint, and rosemary. Other favorites are flowers that have flat surfaces that can be used for landing pads, such as calendula, coreopsis, aster, spreading fleabane, zinnia, and Mexican sunflower.

Milkweeds and passionvine are surefire butterfly attractants in desert gardens. Milkweed provides nectar and is also a host plant for both monarch and queen butterflies. Although monarchs are not common here, queens are frequently in flight from spring through fall. Try pine leaf milkweed (*Asclepias linaria*), desert milkweed (*A. subulata*) or butterfly weed (*A. tuberosa*) to encourage their presence. Passionvine is the favored host plant of the gulf fritillary, a showy reddish-orange butterfly common to the Southwest.

Black swallowtail larvae feed on both leaves and flowers of dill, parsley, and fennel. These herbs grow easily in low desert gardens, so plant a few extra for the caterpillars. Giant swallowtail larvae are most often seen on citrus trees. Called "orange dogs," these caterpillars resemble bird droppings, nature's way of camouflaging them from hungry predators.

Encouraging Lizards, Frogs, Toads & Bats

These creatures eat large quantities of insects—a real bonus for gardeners. Lizards like to sun themselves on block walls, and tree lizards will sun on wooden fences. It is fairly easy to attract them to your yard by planting vines on the walls to provide shelter. Try to prevent their urban predators—cats and dogs—from hanging around their territories. Small rock piles with several inches of sand underneath will provide a safe place to hatch their young.

Frogs and toads need a water source to breed. Creating a habitat for them can be problematic in the arid Southwest. They can survive near artificial lakes if there's not too much wave action or if there's still water near a patch of cattails, for example. The spadefoot toad has adapted to breed in small areas of water and you may see them in late summer with the arrival of the monsoon thunderstorms in the low desert. They must dig down into moist soil for hibernation.

Bat houses are often recommended to attract these interesting mammals, although according to Joe Yarchin of Arizona Game & Fish, there's not much evidence that they use the houses in the low desert because of the extreme heat. (For the same reason, few birds set up residence in birdhouses.) At higher elevations, however, bat houses are a good idea if you want to encourage bats to visit your landscape.

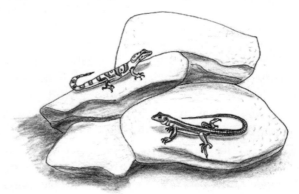

Encourage lizards to live in your yard and they will consume cockroaches and crickets for you. Rock piles provide a place for lizards to sun themselves and shelter to hatch and raise their young.

What About Unwelcome Visitors?

Depending on where you live, you may receive visits from a range of wildlife that you don't want, such as rodents, rabbits, javelina, snakes, and at higher elevations, deer and elk. These creatures all play an important part in the Southwest's ecosystem, although not all of them are suitable in backyard habitats. They may be a nuisance or, in some cases, dangerous. They may eat more of your plant material than you can tolerate, especially in times of drought when native vegetation is sparse and parched. The Arizona Game & Fish Department discourages supplemental feeding of large mammals (skunks, raccoons, and larger mammals) as it is detrimental to their long-term health and survival. They require larger areas for living space than urban environments can accommodate and not all residents would appreciate having them in the neighborhood. "They can also become too accustomed to humans and lose their fear while expecting to be fed," explains Joe Yarchin from Arizona Game & Fish.

Ironically, one of the steps to discourage these unwanted visitors is to remove the elements that make up a viable backyard wildlife habitat. In other words, eliminate sources of water, food, and shelter for a particular species. That may be difficult to do; the only sure-fire method to keep out unwelcome animals is to erect some type of barrier, either around an area or individual desirable plants.

Following is a list of free publications produced by the University of Arizona Cooperative Extension or the Arizona Game & Fish Department that provide information on managing specific species. University publications may be downloaded from the website listed or obtained from County Cooperative Extension offices. Game & Fish publications may be obtained from their offices around the state. (See Resources for office locations.) If you reside elsewhere with different problem species, contact your state's game and fish or wildlife department. The Arizona Game & Fish Department website (www.gf.state.az.us) provides links to similar agencies in all states.

University of Arizona Cooperative Extension publications
Deer and Rabbit Resistant Plants. http://ag.arizona.edu/pubs/garden/az1237.pdf
Javelina Resistant Plants. http://ag.arizona.edu/pubs/garden/az1238.pdf
Roof Rat Control around Homes and Other Structures. http://ag.arizona.edu/pubs/insects/az1280.pdf
Chipmunks, Ground Squirrels, Pocket Gophers. http://ag.arizona.edu/urbanipm/vertebrates.html

Arizona Game & Fish publications
Be Bear Aware
Elk and the Homeowner: A Problem Solving Guide
Living With Arizona's Wildlife: The Raccoon
Living With Arizona's Wildlife: The Skunk
Living With Arizona's Wildlife: Urban Ducks
Living With Arizona's Wildlife: Urban Javelina
Living With Mountain Lions in Arizona
The Urban Coyote

Selecting Plants for Edible Landscapes

When deciding what to plant, your thoughts may first turn to a typical landscape with trees and shrubs and perhaps a patch of turf for the kids to play on. For a refreshing change of pace—and taste—install at least some of your landscape with edible plants. Edibles are fantastic multipurpose plants, as they can provide color, fragrance, shade, screening, as well as fresh, flavorful food for your table.

In her influential book, *The Complete Book of Edible Landscaping*, Rosalind Creasy writes eloquently on the value of replacing at least some strictly ornamental plants with those that provide us with sustenance and a connection to the soil—a connection that has been mostly lost since World War II and society's move from a rural to an urban or suburban locale. She provides an historical perspective on changes in landscape design (until fairly recently in human history, only the wealthy could afford plants for purely ornamental uses), as well as current economic and environmental advantages for returning edible plants to our yards.

Regardless of your reason for doing so, once you begin growing fruits and vegetables, you'll be too spoiled by the sweet fresh flavors to turn back! Here are a few ideas to get you started. These are not the only edible plants available but this information will help expand your notion of what constitutes a landscape plant.

Vegetables, Herbs, and Flowers

Many newcomers to the low desert think that gardening is difficult or impossible because conditions are so different from "back home." In reality, a bountiful harvest of vegetables can be grown easily in the low desert. According to the Arizona Department of Agriculture, Arizona ranks third in the nation for the overall production of fresh vegetables. It is helpful to understand that the low desert has two distinct growing periods—a cool season and a warm season—with different vegetables, flowers, or herbs thriving in each. This is quite different from most parts of the country where one growing season extends through the summer, ending with frost in the fall.

The cool season in the low desert runs from approximately late-September/mid-October through April/May. Annuals are planted from September to February and continue growing until temperatures increase. At that time, annual plants go to seed and die. Warm-season planting starts in mid- to late-February (with added frost protection) to mid-March. Some warm-season plants thrive through the summer's heat; others perform well until the heat hits, then slack off or require extra attention, such as afternoon shade protection. Warm-season plants end their growth cycle when cold temperatures arrive. Of course, weather conditions vary each year so planting dates can be adjusted as needed. *(Desert Gardening for Beginners*, Arizona Master Gardener Press, contains calenders with the best months to plant vegetables, flowers, and herbs.)

Eating flowers may be unfamiliar to you, but edible blossoms are appearing more frequently in trendy restaurant salads and gourmet produce sections. Most common edible flowers grow during the low desert's

---

Rabbit Control

Rabbits especially like young tender growth. To deter them, install larger plants (a five-gallon brittlebush instead of a one-gallon) and put chicken wire around each plant until they are large enough to withstand browsing, usually one growing season.

---

cool-season, including nasturium, calendula, pansy, viola, Johnny-jump-up, dianthus, chrysanthemum, and 'Lemon Gem' or 'Tangerine Gem' signet marigold. Many vegetable, fruit, and herb flowers are edible. Consider trying mint, chives, sage, oregano, okra, squash blossoms, borage, lavender, marjoram, pineapple sage, rosemary, scented geranium, society garlic, broccoli, bok choy, cilantro, dill, and lemon and orange blossoms.

Here are a few pointers before you begin grazing in your flower bed. Not all flowers are edible, and some are poisonous. Consult a good reference book to determine which flowers or flower parts are safe to eat. If you're unsure, don't eat it. Harvest flowers early in the morning for optimum taste. Remove stamens and styles, as well as the white portion at the base of petals, which can be bitter. Wash the blossoms in cool water, wrap in a moist paper towel, and store in the refrigerator to use later that day. Flowers can vary widely in flavor, depending on growing conditions. Don't eat flowers if chemicals have been sprayed.

Many gardeners are familiar with standard culinary herbs such as parsley, sage, oregano, basil, rosemary, and thyme (all of which thrive here). Other herbaceous plants are becoming increasingly popular in the low desert and make interesting additions to the landscape, such as scented geraniums, Mount Lemmon marigold, lavender, Jerusalem sage, artemisia, and lemon grass.

Berries

Blackberries thrive and produce prolifically, but they are rampantly invasive so situate them where that won't be a problem. For example, the varieties that do well in the low desert have thorns, so they can double as a security hedge, especially if your property borders an alley. Their aggressive growth will be stymied on the alley's side, so you should only have to manage their spread on your property.

Fruit yield increases each year as the plants mature. Leaves turn color in the fall, and spring brings white blossoms. Blackberries have few, if any, pest or disease problems in the low desert, although pruning is required to maximize production. Raspberries are a similar bramble (berry and ramble) fruit but they aren't well-acclimated to low desert growing conditions and aren't recommended.

Strawberries make an interesting "groundcover" as the plants send out runners and quickly fill in a space with foliage. Grow them in garden soil amended with plenty of organic matter.

Grapevines bear fruit in the low desert, although they have problems that must be managed. Grape leaf skeletonizers will voraciously decimate the foliage if gardeners don't stay ahead of them. Grapes need to grow in full sun to produce fruit. Full sun reduces the likelihood of powdery mildew. This fungal disease is lessened if there is good air circulation around the plants. Some gardeners are disappointed that homegrown grapes are often the size of the tip of a pinky finger. Commercial growers use hormones and girdling to achieve those thumb-sized grapes. These hormones are not available for homeowner use and girdling techniques require precision and special training. If not done precisely, the vine will die. Girdling removes a continuous strip of plant tissue around the trunk.

Earth-Friendly Gardener

Mike Hills, Master Gardener and past president of the Arizona Herb Association, grows numerous herbaceous plants, both in improved garden soil and the landscape. One of his favorites is *Tagetes lucida*, which is known by many common names, including Mexican mint marigold, root beer plant, Mexican tarragon, and yerba anis. These descriptive names provide hints about the plant's fragrance and culinary uses. "I cut off a couple stems and put them in a container of sun tea," says Hills. "They add a spicy, light licorice, root beer flavor to the tea." The foliage is also used for tarragon flavor in chicken, fish, and egg dishes. The flowers are edible and perk up green salads. He suggests planting this herb next to a walkway where brushing against it releases the scent.

Its purpose is to inhibit transport of sugars from the foliage to the roots; instead girdling "traps" that energy for the fruit. On the plus side, your small grapes will be sweet, grapevines create shade over ramadas, and the dried vines can be used for craft projects.

Citrus Trees

The bright orange or yellow fruits and glossy green leaves of citrus trees are visually stimulating and the dense foliage can screen unsightly views. Citrus trees also provide shade, sweet fragrance when in bloom, fresh fruit and juice, nectar for pollinators, and food and shelter for wildlife. Of course, handpicked citrus from your backyard makes a great holiday gift for relatives shivering in other parts of the country. There are dozens of citrus varieties that are ready to eat in different months. Consider planting several types to extend your harvest period as long as possible. Citrus trees require fertilizer applications three times annually and consistent deep watering throughout the year to remain healthy and produce good fruit.

Deciduous Fruit Trees

Some deciduous fruit trees, such as peaches, plums, apricots, and apples, will produce in the low desert. They require a dormant period of cold temperatures—called chilling hours—before they can develop flowers and set fruit. A chilling hour is defined as one hour at temperatures below 45 degrees Fahrenheit. Some fruit varieties require as many as 1000 chilling hours; others as few as 100 hours. It is essential to choose varieties that fall within the range of chilling hours where you live.

Low desert areas average 300–400 chilling hours per year. (Check with your County Cooperative Extension office for the average in your specific area.) Since temperature fluctuations are always possible from year to year, planting varieties with even lower chilling requirements, such as 250 hours, will provide a higher likelihood of fruit set each year. However, be aware that a fruit tree that needs few chilling hours can start blooming in late winter and be very susceptible to frost damage. If freezing temperatures are predicted, be prepared to cover and protect a tree that blooms early.

To develop fruit, pollen transfers from the male part of the flower to the female part. Nature dictates that some fruit varieties need to be cross-pollinated with another variety, so you would need to plant a second tree nearby. Other varieties can pollinate themselves. These varieties are called self-pollinating or self-fruitful. Before purchasing, determine if the tree requires cross-pollination with another tree. In small backyards, a self-fruitful tree is a good choice.

Fruit trees provide spring bloom and colorful fall foliage. The fruit quality and flavor may be below your expectations. These trees require a regular pruning and fertilizing program to enhance fruit production so they may not be the best choice if you prefer a low-maintenance landscape.

Earth-Friendly Gardener

Master Gardener Carol Brecker enclosed her vegetable and fruit garden in a wood and chicken wire structure to protect plants from the birds and rabbits. "We hated fighting with netting over the fruit trees so we planted a peach, apricot, plum, and fig within the structure," explains Carol. "We are training the trees for width rather than height."

Some Unusual Edible Landscape Plants

Globe Artichokes

Whether you choose to eat the fruit or let it go to flower, this perennial plant is an eye-catcher in the landscape. It has striking silvery foliage with deeply lobed leaves. The mature plant can reach three to four feet tall and wide. The young flower bud is the green, succulent artichoke that we savor when dipped in melted butter. If left to mature on the plant, the artichoke bud will turn into a softball-sized, bluish-purple flower that looks like a thistle, smells like honey, and makes a terrific long-lasting cut or dried flower. Artichokes are best transplanted from January 15 through March 15. During summer, the plant will die back to the ground to escape the heat but will reappear with fall's cooler weather as long as the soil doesn't dry out.

Kumquats

Kumquats are citrus fruits that are eaten whole in one bite. These small fruits have a sweet rind and pulp that is described as sour, spicy, or tart. It provides quite a burst of flavors for the palate. Like most citrus, the bright orange fruit against the dark green foliage creates a pleasing color contrast and flowers are sweetly fragrant. Kumquats are a small, compact tree (6 to 12 feet tall) and can perform in limited spaces, containers, and even as shrubs. Try to place them where you can enjoy the scent wafting through an open window. They need full sun, but are more cold hardy than other citrus because they are in a different genus.

Devil's Claw

Devil's claw is a native that thrives through the summer heat and provides a variety of unusual functions. It grows about two to three feet wide and tall and has soft, attractive foliage. It produces a pretty orchid-like flower with a white and pink or rosy-purplish hue. The green fruit pod looks and tastes somewhat like okra. It must be eaten when it is young and pliable as it becomes woody and unpalatable as it ages. When completely dry, the pod will split open in the shape of a claw. The fibers from the claws are used in traditional Native American basketmaking. Pulling the claws apart will expose seeds with an outer shell. Remove this shell to find edible seeds that resemble sunflower seeds. Devil's claw doesn't survive freezing temperatures, but it will reseed itself. Seeds usually germinate with the summer monsoon rains.

Chiltepines

These native chiles grow wild in southern Arizona, usually under a "nurse plant" such as a mesquite tree, which provides filtered light and protection from the hot sun. Their pea-sized fruits pack a wallop of heat. Chiltepines often live longer than many hybridized chile plants and reach greater sizes. They start producing fruits around May and bear white flowers, green peppers, and red peppers at the same time, which creates a vibrant picture in the landscape. They can fruit through much of the summer, as well as produce another crop in the fall. Chiltepines are the perfect, "user-friendly chile." Their size is perfect for one serving of soup, stew, or eggs, with no measuring or chopping required.

Keyhole Beds and Spiral Gardens

Keyhole beds and spiral gardens are fun and attractive ways to save space in the garden. Called "keyhole" and "spiral" because their layout resembles those shapes, these gardens maximize the use of limited space and provide better access to the plants for the gardener. Both keyhole and spiral gardens work well for salad or kitchen gardens.

Keyhole beds. One or more short paths shaped like a keyhole either radiate from a central point or jut off from a main path. If you stand or kneel within the "keyhole," it allows you to work most of the bed without walking on the soil, thus reducing compaction.

Spiral gardens. These are small rock gardens built in the shape of a spiral. They are three dimensional, having height as well as length and width. Spiral gardens are usually higher in the middle and lower on the outside edges.

Selecting Plants for Low-Allergen Gardens

Allergies are on the rise in the United States. In 1959, two to five percent of the population suffered from them. In 1984, the number was 12–15 percent and it spiked to 38 percent in 1999 according to Thomas Ogren, author of *Allergy-Free Gardening: The Revolutionary Guide to Healthy Landscaping*. He attributes these increases to two major changes in our landscaping practices: the exclusive use of male plants and installing monocultures. Plant breeders developed male clones to avoid the cleanup required with seedpod- or fruit-producing female plants. However, male plants produce prodigious amounts of pollen causing allergy symptoms when the microscopic grains are inhaled. Although monocultures—mass groupings of the same plant—may be aesthetically pleasing, they greatly increase the opportunity to be overexposed to a particular allergen. If one tree can produce millions of pollen grains, think what an urban development or freeway planted entirely in the same species will produce.

It is impossible to control pollen grains that drift in from surrounding neighborhoods, but you can choose low-allergenic plants for your landscape. Even if you don't suffer from allergies, alleviating some of the misery for those who do by planting low-allergen plants qualifies as a component of permaculture's Care of the People defined in Chapter 1. Because there's no guarantee that you or your children won't develop allergies in the future, choose low-allergen plants now. To guide your plant selection, it helps to understand how allergies develop and how the pollination process can influence your symptoms.

Allergies and Pollen

To develop an allergy, several things have to happen. "First, your body must have the genetic make-up to be susceptible to a specific plant," explains Mary Kay O'Rourke, Associate Professor of Public Health Research for the University of Arizona College of Public Health. Second, you need to be exposed to a "threshold dose" of that plant's pollen. The threshold dose is not the same for everyone and it can change for a person through time. Third, you must be repeatedly exposed to the plant. Finally, the more frequent your exposure to the plant, the greater the allergic reaction becomes. "And, just because you are not allergic to something today, doesn't mean that you won't develop an allergy over time, as you are exposed to the plant," O'Rourke cautions.

Plant Pollination

Most plants are primarily pollinated by either living creatures or by the wind, although some are pollinated by both methods. Flowers have developed differently depending on their primary pollination method. Brightly colored, showy flowers attract birds, moths, bats, bees, and numerous insect pollinators. The blossoms may be fragrant and are situated prominently on the plant. The pollen grains are usually sticky and highly ornamental with spines and bumps to facilitate attachment to the pollinator as it moves among plants. The male parts of the flower are often tucked within the blossom so that insects must crawl inside to do their work.

Colorful showy flowers that are pollinated by bees and other insects are less likely to cause allergies than non-descript flowers that are wind-pollinated.

53

Take a moment to observe this process in your garden. Follow a busy bee's path as it dives into a flower. When it emerges, its tiny body resembles a dust cloth covered in specks of pollen. The bee obligingly carries this along for the ride from flower to flower.

Wind-pollinated plants, on the other hand, usually have small, nondescript flowers. Many are thin, hanging flower clusters that are an inch or so long. Their color is often a rather unnoticeable pale white or greenish-yellow shade. Because the wind is less precise than insects or other creatures, these plants produce copious amounts of pollen to increase the chances of successful pollination. In the Southwest's dry, windy climate, this pollen can be transported quite a distance and remain aloft for an extended period. The pollen grains are small, light, and non-sticky, making them easily airborne, and unfortunately, easily inhaled. Rain and humidity greatly reduce the pollen grains' windborne travels. The same allergy-guilty tree in the low desert might be of little consequence in Seattle or New Orleans with their rain and humidity. This might explain why mulberry trees in Georgia are not considered much of a pollen issue, whereas they are a significant problem in the low desert.

A plant's reproductive process can influence the amount of pollen in the air. Some plants have "complete" flowers, which contain both male and female reproductive parts. The anther (male) contains pollen, which needs to be transferred to the stigma (female) so that ultimately fruits and seeds can be produced. Other plants have some flowers with all female parts and other flowers with all male parts on the same plant. In still other plants, there are male plants that have only male flowers and female plants that have only female flowers. The male plant is pollen-bearing and the female plant is fruit-bearing. These single-sexed plants are usually wind-pollinated. To ensure pollination, lots of pollen has to be produced. In the last few decades, homeowners and landscapers wanted to avoid the clean-up associated with so-called "messy" fruiting trees, so only the male of the species was propagated and planted. In some cases, this practice has back-fired because the high pollen production of the male wasn't factored in as an undesirable trait.

The male flowers and female flowers of jojoba appear on separate plants. The female develops the small brown fruit.

Opuntia cacti have complete flowers, containing both male and female reproductive parts. Complete flowers are usually not a significant allergen problem because the pollen doesn't have far to travel.

Reduce Your Landscape's Allergen Potential

If you are unsure of a plant's allergy potential, examine its flowers to determine the most likely method of pollination. Plants with big showy flowers are generally pollinated by insects and are usually not as significant a factor in allergies as wind-pollinated plants. Many annual vegetables, flowers, and bulbs do not create significant problems. However, if your allergies are severe, choose trumpet-shaped flowers (salvia, penstemon) or flowers that enclose the male parts (snapdragon) to reduce pollen exposure. Plant females instead of males if appropriate.

Create a diverse garden with many plant species. Although monocultures are less of a problem in the home landscape than in community-wide projects, plant diversity helps guard against high dose exposures to any particular allergen. Even a plant with limited allergen potential can become a problem when planted in great quantity.

Choose plants that are well-adapted for your area and maintain them properly. Stressed plants are attacked by pests, such as aphids, which produce honeydew. Mold quickly grows on the nutrient-rich honeydew and mold spores are allergenic. Also, a stressed male plant will put out two to three times as much pollen before it dies in an attempt to reproduce itself, according to author Thomas Ogren.

Mature trees will produce enormous amounts of pollen in comparison to shrubs and perennials. Although the shade is welcome, consider replacing such trees with a lower pollen-producing species.

Common or improved Bermudagrass grown from seed is a major contributor to the pollen count. Mow lawns frequently enough to reduce the height of flowering stalks or plant sterile vegetative hybrid Bermuda that doesn't produce flowers or pollen. Regular mowing keeps the flower stalks closer to the ground, reducing the amount of pollen the wind carries with it. Taller flower stalks allow the wind to readily transport the pollen.

What about native plants versus introduced species? Years ago, physicians sent patients who suffered from respiratory ailments to Southwestern deserts for relief. Recently, the prevailing wisdom has been that the enormous variety of non-native plants introduced over the years as the population grew contributed to an increase in allergy and asthma cases. However, both native and non-native species can cause allergies. Ironically, a Phoenix physician by the name of E.W. Phillips was publishing articles as far back as the 1920s, describing the allergies that his patients suffered from the native bursage plant and urging doctors not to send their allergic patients to the area.

Tips to Reduce Allergy Problems While Gardening

Wear a dust mask, goggles, gloves, and a long-sleeved shirt.

Shower and launder immediately after gardening.

Close windows when the lawn is being mowed and keep them closed for several hours after.

Don't use air blowers to "clean up" sidewalks and driveways. These blowers stir up particulates.

Many weeds are major pollen producers. Pull weeds immediately before they can flower and go to seed.

Limit outdoor activity between 5 and 10 a.m. when pollen and mold counts are highest, as well as on hot, dry windy days.

High-Allergen Plants to Avoid

Check with your city or county for plant restrictions. Many jurisdictions have implemented "pollen ordinances" that prohibit the planting of some species, such as male mulberry and most olive trees. Individuals can have widely varying tolerances to different plants, including skin problems caused by direct contact with plant tissue or reactions to flowers with fragrances. Consult a doctor or allergy specialist for your condition.

The book, *Allergy-Free Gardening: The Revolutionary Guide to*

High-Allergen Plant List

Arizona ash (male)
Fraxinus velutina

Arizona cypress
Cupressus arizonica

Canyon ragweed/giant
bursage
Ambrosia ambrosioides

Common or improved
Bermudagrass

Fruitless mulberry (male)
Morus alba

Hop bush
Dodonaea viscosa

Italian cypress
Cupressus sempervirens

Juniper (male)
Juniperus sp.

Mesquite
Prosopis sp.

Fruiting olive
Olea europaea
(However, there are trade-
marked pollenless varieties.)

Saltbush
Atriplex sp.

Sumac
Rhus sp.

Triangleleaf bursage/rabbit
bush
Ambrosia deltoidea

Healthy Landscaping, categorizes thousands of plants on a scale from 1 to 10, with 1 having the least amount of pollen and related allergy problems (including asthma) and 10 having the most.

The best protection is to know what you are allergic to and minimize exposure to the plant. Try to keep the worst offenders out of your landscape. The plants in the adjacent list typically cause the most allergic reactions and are often found in Arizona landscapes.

Selecting Plants for Wildfire-Defensible Landscapes

There is no such thing as a fire-proof plant, but some are more resistant than others. After reviewing the design suggestions in Chapter 2, consider the following characteristics when choosing plants for a wildfire-defensible landscape.

Select landscape plants with a high moisture content, which is the most important characteristic determining flammability. These include succulents and some herbaceous plants. Also, deciduous species (those that drop their leaves) tend to have foliage with a higher moisture content.

Avoid evergreen trees and shrubs that have a high resin (pitch) content, which makes them more flammable. These include junipers, firs, pines, spruces, Arizona cypress, and other conifers.

Plant groundcovers in lieu of grass. Many groundcovers are succulent. They also provide erosion control, inhibit weeds, and reduce maintenance chores.

If you live at higher elevations near a natural water source, deciduous trees such as aspen and cottonwood are fire-resistant. However, they are not drought-tolerant species and struggle without adequate water. ✳

Chapter 4

Plant Care

Observing your plants on a regular basis and maintaining them with proper cultural techniques are key steps for growing a healthy, earth-friendly landscape. Maintaining healthy plants is more rewarding than frequently intervening with various "fixes" whenever problems arise. This chapter will explain how to effectively water, mulch, compost, fertilize, and prune. Following these plant care guidelines will help you save time and money while nurturing healthy plants.

Observation: Early Detection and Intervention

Stay on top of the situation. Walk around your landscape at least once a week. Initially you may feel too busy—this is just one more chore on an already long list of to-dos. But stick with it and you will probably look forward to this connection with your natural surroundings as a welcome respite from other pressures. A variety of interesting research studies have demonstrated the benefits of contact with nature. Even indirect contact, in which subjects looked at natural scenes but had no interaction with plants or the outdoors, displayed significant results. One hospital study found that patients who enjoyed a view of trees from their window used less pain medication and had shorter stays than patients who had to stare at a brick wall. A study of prison inmates found those whose cells looked out on farm land had fewer sick calls than those who faced the prison's bleak court-yard. Imagine the positive benefits you will receive activating all of your senses in the garden.

As you spend time observing your plants, you will learn what they typically look like and be attuned to any changes. This puts you in a perfect position to halt problems before they get out of control. It is much easier to make small adjustments in a plant's care regimen than handle a full-blown pest invasion on a weakened plant.

The healthiest plants are the most pest resistant. "A healthy plant is not a prime target for insects," explains Terry Mikel, University of Arizona Cooperative Extension Commercial Horticulture Agent. "If a healthy plant does get attacked, it possesses a whole series of reactions to stop, repel, isolate, and actively attack an invader, be it insect or disease." Maintaining healthy, stress-free plants is the best way to prevent problems.

Watering

Watering correctly will benefit your plants more than any other care you can provide. Effective watering is so crucial that when people call the University of Arizona Maricopa County Cooperative Extension Master Gardener Hotline with plant problems, the first question the Master Gardener volunteer usually asks is, "How are you watering the plant?" In addition to growing healthy plants, efficient watering promotes an earth-friendly landscape. Overwatering wastes groundwater resources, and excess runoff causes soil erosion. Overwatering can leach pollutants into our water supply, which will be discussed in more detail in a later section on fertilizing.

With extended periods of drought around much of the country, as well as restrictions placed on landscape watering, it is important to water efficiently to conserve water and keep your plants alive.

"How much water should I apply?" "How often should I water?" The topic of watering seems to generate more questions from gardeners than any other. Even people in the industry may provide differing answers because there are so many factors involved. What type of plant is it? When was it planted? How old is it? How big is it? What kind of soil is it growing in? Is it in sun or shade? What is the air temperature? Is there any wind? What is the unique microclimate at your location? It would be difficult for any expert to provide an easy, one-answer-fits-all response that would work in all landscapes.

That's why it is important to master three easy concepts that will allow you to water efficiently no matter where you live or what type of plants you have. Understanding these points will take away reliance on the experts and put you in charge of conserving water in your landscape regardless of the irrigation system you use. First, the water should run long enough to soak through the root zone to the appropriate depth. Second, water should be applied where the roots are able to absorb it. Third, there should be time between waterings to allow the soil to dry out. An easy way to remember this is to: Water Deep, Water Wide, and Water Infrequently.

When is the Best Time to Water Lawns?

Run lawn sprinklers from 3 a.m. to 6 a.m. to reduce loss from evaporation. As much as 30 percent of water is lost if applied during the hot midday sun. If it is also windy, 50 percent of water is wasted.

Water Deep

Water should soak deeply enough to moisten the plant's root system and to leach away harmful salts. An easy way to remember how deep to water is the 1-2-3 Rule. Plants with shallow root systems need water to reach 1 foot deep. These include perennials, groundcovers, annual flowers and vegetables, herbs, cacti, and succulents. Shrubs should be watered to a depth of 2 feet. Trees have deeper root systems and water should soak 3 feet deep. (Turf doesn't quite fit into the 1-2-3 Rule. Bermudagrass should be watered to a depth of 8-10 inches. Winter ryegrass has a shorter

The 1-2-3 Rule is an easy way to remember how deep to water plants: Water should penetrate 1 foot deep for annuals, small shrubs, groundcovers, cacti, and other succulents, 2 feet deep for shrubs, and 3 feet deep for trees. Use a soil probe to determine how far water has soaked into the soil.

root system and water should penetrate 4-6 inches.)

How do you determine how far water has soaked? It is easy with a soil probe. Any long, pointed piece of metal will work. For example, some gardeners buy a length of rebar (which usually costs less than a dollar) and sharpen it. A handle welded to the probe makes it easier to push in and pull out of the soil. Some nurseries and Cooperative Extension offices may offer soil probes for sale. After watering, push the soil probe into the soil. It will move relatively easily through moist soil and stop when it hits dry, hard soil. Compare how far the water has penetrated with how long the irrigation was running and make adjustments as needed. Since water will continue to infiltrate through the soil even after the irrigation or hose has been shut off, wait a couple hours before using the probe to get a more accurate reading. Also note that water will penetrate differently in different soil types. In clay soil, it spreads in a wide shallow pattern; in sandy soil it moves in a narrow, deep pattern. Loam soil is somewhere between the two.

In addition to wetting the root ball, another reason to water deeply is to prevent salt burn. Desert soils and water supplies contain a lot of salts. You have probably seen white, crusty salt deposits on top of the soil ringing watering wells or around the edges of container plants. When salts accumulate in a plant's root zone, they reduce its ability to uptake water and nutrients and cause "salt burn." Salt burn first appears as yellowing leaves, usually around the edges of the foliage. Leaves may continue to brown, curl up, and drop off. If the condition continues without correction, the plant may die.

Salt is soluble in water, which allows it to move through the soil along with the water during irrigation. Wherever the water stops penetrating is where the salt will be deposited. Watering deeply leaches the salts below the root zone. It is not a good practice to run the drip irrigation system for 15-20 minutes or sprinkle around plants lightly with a hose. This contributes to salt build-up because such a small output of water can not penetrate deeply.

Water Wide

"Feeder roots" actively take up moisture and nutrients to distribute through the entire plant. Feeder roots are at the tips of the root system, whether it is a tree, shrub, or smaller plant. They are actively pushing onward through the soil. Water should be applied where these feeder roots are growing. As a general guideline, feeder roots are aligned with the outer edge of a plant's canopy and may spread up to four times as wide. If you use a drip system, emitters need to be moved outward as the plant grows. For larger plants, add more emitters spaced evenly around the circumference. If you fill a watering well with a hose, the berms of the watering well should be moved outward. If you use a garden hose, drag it out further.

Water Infrequently

Your goal is to apply water as infrequently as possible. This is im-

Earth-Friendly Gardener

Master Gardener Sue Hakala practices water conservation by spot-watering specific smaller plants that require additional moisture. This eliminates the need to run the irrigation system for extra time. "I poke a small hole in a one-gallon milk jug, fill it with water, and put it near the plant so it gets watered slowly and deeply," explains Sue. This method also prevents the more drought-tolerant plants from being overwatered, which would make them susceptible to root rot or other problems.

portant to both conserve water and to maintain healthy plants. Surprisingly, overwatering is as big a problem in the desert as underwatering, probably because gardeners overcompensate for living in such arid conditions. Roots need oxygen to thrive or they may rot. If soil is constantly wet, the oxygen has been forced out of the spaces between soil particles and replaced by water. Overwatering also encourages plants to grow aggressively, requiring more pruning and maintenance. Native and desert-adapted plants actually thrive with minimal water, as that is what they have adapted to over the ages.

Underwatering is harmful as it stresses the plant, causing it to wilt. If it goes too long without sufficient water, it may not recover. Watch plants for signs of underwatering stress and irrigate before plants reach this state. As a further guideline, when the top one-half to one-third of the root zones (using the 1-2-3 Rule) dries out, plants may need water.

One of the best—and easiest—steps you can take to conserve water is to adjust the timer on your automatic irrigation monthly with the changes in temperature. Leave the length of time that the system runs the same: this ensures the water will penetrate the appropriate depth. It is the frequency with which water is applied that is either increased with warm weather or decreased with cool weather.

Mulching and Composting

Using mulch and compost in your landscape will enhance plant vigor and at the same time significantly reduce yard waste sent to overflowing landfills. According to U.S. Environmental Protection Agency (EPA) statistics from 1999 (the most recent year available), Americans generated a mountain of garbage—229 million tons. Yard trimmings accounted for 12.1 percent of that total—27.7 million tons. These figures are averaged over the entire country for the entire year. Regions with year-around growing conditions, such as the low desert, generate a larger percentage of yard waste. During summer months, when most homeowners maintain lawns

Signs of Underwatering Stress

✓ Leaves wilt, droop, or curl.

✓ Foliage appears dull, rather than glossy or shiny.

✓ Older leaves (lower on the plant) turn yellow and brown, eventually dropping off.

✓ Entire stems or branches dry and die back.

Apply water at the outer edge of a plant's canopy where the feeder roots are growing. One emitter is usually sufficient for small plants. Shrubs and trees need more emitters spaced evenly around the perimeter so the expanding root zone receives water.

or gardens, the percentage of yard waste rises to as much as 50 percent of the total refuse trucked to landfills.

As an encouraging trend, the EPA study showed that total yard waste had been reduced from 1992's total of 35 million tons. The drop was attributed to increased state and local regulations that either limit the amount of landscape trimmings that can be sent to landfills or charge higher fees for disposal. Being hit in the pocketbook encouraged alternatives, such as mulching mowers and composting.

Source reduction, also referred to as waste prevention, is the preferred method for dealing with yard waste. It simply means reducing the volume of trimmings your yard generates by smart plant selection and using what trimmings are generated on-site, rather than sending green waste to the landfill. The following practices will help you significantly reduce landscape waste, and at the same time, improve the health of your plants by adding nutrients to the soil.

- ❑ Apply mulch on soil, pathways, and around plants.
- ❑ Leave grass clippings on the lawn, called grasscycling.
- ❑ Make compost.

Benefits of Mulch

Mulching is simply covering the soil with a layer of organic or inorganic matter. Mulch provides a variety of important benefits. It maintains soil moisture by reducing evaporation. A Texas A&M University study found that unmulched soil loses twice as much water to evaporation as mulched soil. It inhibits weed growth by preventing sunlight from reaching the weed seeds, preventing germination. Mulch reduces soil erosion and compaction. It keeps fruits and vegetables from touching wet soil, reducing damage and rot. And, a layer of mulch can visually enhance the landscape.

Inorganic Mulch

Decomposed granite is an example of an inorganic mulch that is often spread on Southwestern landscapes. Granite serves the basic purposes of mulch listed above and does not require frequent replacement. However, it does not add nutrients or improve soil structure. Plant litter will show, creating a situation in which it must be constantly removed if you want a "clean" look. Plastic is not recommended as a mulch as it inhibits or prevents water and oxygen penetration into the soil and encourages root systems to grow close to the soil surface. Geotextiles (also called landscape fabric or synthetic mulch) are porous, although weed seeds can accumulate on top of the material and germinate anyway. Roots can penetrate geotextiles, which makes it more difficult to remove the material without damaging root systems. Thus, they are not effective in garden beds or areas where shallow-rooted groundcovers are grown.

Earth-Friendly Gardener

Consulting Rosarian Alan Zelhart has found another use for mulch with his container plants. "I place a five-gallon plastic pot with plants into a larger decorative wooden pot," describes Alan. "Then I fill the cavity between the two with mulch and finally cover the soil surface of the planted pot with mulch." This technique keeps the containers cool and reduces evaporation so Alan doesn't have to water as frequently.

Organic Mulch

Organic mulches offer other benefits that make them a better choice than inorganic mulches for many gardeners. Adding a layering of organic mulch is one of the easiest things you can do to produce healthy plants and an earth-friendly landscape. Organic mulches slowly break down over time, replenishing nutrients and improving soil structure. They provide "food" for beneficial soil organisms and worms who work around the clock building soil. Organic mulches moderate soil temperature, keeping it cooler in summer and warmer in winter. They provide an important alternative use for landscape trimmings that would otherwise be sent to the landfills. This in turn increases the lifespan of landfills, many of which are reaching capacity. Organic mulches are aesthetically attractive, adding a natural texture and color to the landscape that mirrors the desert itself.

How to Apply Mulch

Remove existing weeds. Spread two to four inches of organic mulch on pathways and around the base of plants. Generally, a large, coarse material, such as wood chips, is applied more thickly than a small, fine material, such as sawdust or grass clippings. Granite mulches don't need to be applied as thickly, usually about one to a maximum of two inches.

Mulch should extend at least six inches beyond the edge of the plant's canopy where root tips are actively growing. Leave 6–10 inches of bare ground surrounding the stem or trunk. This helps prevent wet mulch from contacting bark or stem tissue, which provides a favorable environment for pests and diseases. Organic mulches break down over time, so periodically replenish them.

Sources of Free Mulch

If your yard doesn't generate as much organic mulch as you would like to use, check with utilities and local government agencies responsible for tree trimming, roadside maintenance, and public plantings. Landscape companies and arborists are another possible source. Because they pay a "tipping" fee to use the landfills, they are often willing to drop a truckload if they are already scheduled to be in your neighborhood. Before delivery, specify what you want (e.g., grass clippings or wood chips) and ensure trimmings are not from plants that were sprayed with chemicals.

Another Mulching Method: Grasscycling

"Grasscycling" allows clippings to remain on the lawn and decompose after mowing rather than be collected for disposal. When mowing, tiny bits of grass fall through the lawn's canopy and reach the soil, where they begin decomposing. Mulching lawn mowers have special blades and mower decks that increase the times the clippings tumble around before being discharged. Thus, the grass clippings are cut into smaller pieces than with regular mowers, and they can decompose more quickly. However, traditional mowers can be used if the grass is mowed regularly at the proper frequency and height. Grasscycling is fast gaining favor as the best method of disposal as the clippings return nutrients to the soil and

Organic Mulches

- ✓ compost
- ✓ leaves
- ✓ grass clippings
- ✓ pine needles
- ✓ shredded wood
- ✓ bark chips
- ✓ sawdust
- ✓ hay or straw
- ✓ landscape trimmings
- ✓ chipper/shredder remains
- ✓ cottonseed hulls
- ✓ peanut shells

reduce fertilizer requirements. Equally important, grasscycling eliminates the time and expense required to bag and send clippings to the landfills.

Over time, the additional organic matter provided by the clippings will improve the soil's fertility and water retention capability, resulting in fertilizer and water savings. Clippings may return up to 25 percent nitrogen to the soil, reducing required fertilizer application by a similar amount.

When grasscycling, mow grass frequently enough to maintain its recommended "mowing height." Mowing height is measured from the soil surface to the grass blade's tip immediately after mowing. This height varies depending on the grass species. For example, improved Bermudagrass has a recommended mowing height of one-half to two inches, St. Augustine from two to three inches, and perennial ryegrass from three-fourths to two and one-half inches. If you are installing a new lawn, obtain mowing height recommendations from the nursery or supplier. You can also check with your County Cooperative Extension office for guidelines for your area's typical grass types. Regardless of the height, never mow more than one-third of the grass blade at any time. Removing more than that eliminates essential photosynthesizing tissue and slows root growth.

Grass clippings left on the lawn to decompose do not cause thatch, which is a fibrous layer of organic matter between the surface of the soil and the grass. Thatch is comprised of dead stems, roots, and stolons that build up faster than they can decompose. It was once thought that grass clippings could contribute to thatch build-up, but studies show that this is not the case. Grass clippings are so small that they quickly decompose.

> ## Grasscycling Saves Time
>
> A study of homeowners conducted by Texas A&M University showed that grasscycling required one extra mowing per month, but because the grass was shorter, each mowing took 35 minutes less. After six months, participants saved a total of seven hours.

Compost

Compost is organic matter that has decomposed sufficiently to create a dark brown, crumbly substance with a fresh, earthy smell. Compost can be used as mulch, but many mulches are not broken down enough to be called compost. Humus is a fine, rich organic matter that has reached its final state of decomposition. If you have ever brushed aside a layer of leaves from a forest floor to uncover a rich, dark layer of "soil," you have seen the result of Mother Nature's composting process.

Composting provides a long list of benefits both for your landscape and the environment. Compost makes an excellent mulch to spread around plants and it is a wonderful soil amendment to dig into vegetable and flower beds. It improves drainage and aeration in clay soil. In sandy soil it helps to retain moisture and nutrients. Regular additions of compost will improve soil structure and tilth, a term used to describe soil's "workability." Compost improves fertility in all soils, which reduces the need for synthetic fertilizers. It helps to foster a healthy soil environment where beneficial soil organisms, such as earthworms, bacteria, and fungi, can live.

Composting yard waste and kitchen scraps reduces the amount of waste sent to landfills, while recycling valuable organic matter and nutrients back into the soil. It saves the time, labor, and expense of bagging and hauling it away. Ultimately, healthy soil helps grow healthy plants

Lawn Care Basics

Watering

Turf is healthier if watered only as often as necessary to prevent wilt. Tell-tale signs of wilt include footprints after walking on the grass and a bluish cast to the foliage. Established lawns do not need to be watered daily. That practice wastes water and promotes fungal diseases and a shallow root system. Overwatering encourages excess growth, which requires more frequent mowing and disposal.

Allow the soil surface to dry out between each watering. Water should penetrate through the entire root system with each irrigation. This will promote a stronger, more drought-tolerant lawn. Bermudagrass should be watered 8–10 inches deep. Ryegrass has a more shallow root system so water it only 4–6 inches deep. To determine how far water has penetrated, stick a long-handled screwdriver or soil probe into the ground 30 minutes after watering. The probe will move readily through moist soil and stop at dry soil.

Run sprinklers long enough for water to soak through to the appropriate depth, but not run onto sidewalks and streets. If this occurs, adjust the timer. Program it to apply water for as long as possible without runoff, then stop, allowing time for the water to soak in. Start another watering cycle. Repeat the process until the water reaches the correct depth.

Fertilizing

There are numerous lawn fertilizers on the market and varying recommendations as to what to use and how often to apply it. Monthly fertilizer applications are sufficient for actively growing established lawns. Overfertilizing contributes to contamination from runoff and causes grass to grow "too fast." This in turn requires more frequent mowing, which adds to air pollution.

Nitrogen, which promotes green foliage, is essential for a healthy lawn. A good choice is a complete fertilizer with a 3-1-2 NPK ratio such as 21-7-14 that also contains traces of sulfur, iron, zinc, and magnesium. Ammonium nitrate (33-0-0) and ammonium sulfate (21-0-0) are often recommended to fertilize lawns. Ammonium nitrate should be used in cool weather and ammonium sulfate in warm weather. Apply fertilizer immediately before an irrigation so that the water will wash it off the blades and soak it into the root system.

Mowing

Remove only the top one-third of grass blades each time you mow. Cutting more than that inhibits the plant's ability to photosynthesize and stops root growth. Removing too much can also "scalp" the grass, exposing its growing points, which are at the soil surface (not at the tip of the grass shoots).

Mower blades should always be sharp. Dull blades contribute to an unattractive lawn, as they shred the grass tips, causing them to turn brown. Mow grass when it is dry. Mowing wet grass can spread fungal diseases and create a mess with matted clippings. If clumps are left on the lawn, the grass underneath turns yellow. Wet grass also clings underneath the mower, which can result in more maintenance.

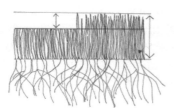

Remove only the top one-third of grass blades each time you mow to reach the recommended "mowing height" for your grass species. Mowing height is measured from the soil surface to the tip of the grass blades immediately after mowing.

that are more resistant to insects and diseases and it reduces reliance on pesticides.

You can purchase compost in large bags or by the truckload or make your own. It is easy to get started with a few pointers. If you purchase compost in bags, be sure it is actually compost and not just shredded organic matter. This is useful as a top mulch but is not the decomposed compost as described here.

Compost Ingredients

There are four basic ingredients for a compost pile: carbon, nitrogen, water, and oxygen. A varied army of microorganisms (bacteria, fungi, microbes, protozoas) and macroorganisms (earthworms, sowbugs, grubs, centipedes) works to break down the organic matter, releasing nutrients in a continuous cycle of death and renewal. These creatures need the same things as we do to survive: food, water, and oxygen. Too much or too little of any of these ingredients will inhibit, but not stop, the decomposition process.

All organic matter contains some carbon and some nitrogen. However, for composting definitions, organic matter is classified as "carbon" or "nitrogen," based on the relative percentage of each that is contained in the material. Most carbon materials are "brown" in color, such as dried leaves, and most nitrogen materials are "green," such as grass clippings. The microorganisms use carbon-rich material for energy and growth; nitrogen is used for growth and reproduction. If a pile runs out of nitrogen, the microorganisms will reproduce more slowly and, in turn, the decomposition process will slow considerably. If an appropriate balance of carbon and nitrogen is present, the composting process will continue in optimal fashion.

The "ideal" compost pile contains a carbon to nitrogen mix of 30:1, in other words 30 parts carbon to 1 part nitrogen. Most of the organisms decomposing the pile prefer more carbon than nitrogen. Try to balance the materials in your compost pile, but don't let the carbon to nitrogen ratios intimidate you—a math degree isn't necessary to make compost. Start with a mix of two-thirds carbon materials and one-third nitrogen materials, (for example, two bags full of dried leaves and one bag full of grass clippings). However, use the very rich carbon materials, such as sawdust or newspaper, sparingly. Although everything will decompose eventually, an overabundance of carbon will slow the process dramatically. If nitrogen materials are scarce, you can always incorporate more later when you turn the pile or add an organic nitrogen fertilizer, such as blood meal. The more variety in your materials, the better.

Common carbon and nitrogen materials used in compost piles, as well as carbon to nitrogen ratios, are listed in the chart on the next page.

Constructing a Compost Pile

The smaller the pieces, the faster they will decompose. Chop or break larger chunks of woody plant material, corn stalks, and branches to create more surface area for the bacteria to enter. Alternate three- or four-

Don't Put These in the Compost Pile

Cat, dog, or pet bird manure, which may contain pathogens that can be transmitted to humans.

Bermudagrass stolons or rhizomes (runners), which can live to sprout another day.

Weed seeds.

Diseased plants.

Fireplace ashes. Ashes are highly alkaline. Southwestern soils are already alkaline and do not need anything that will increase the pH level of the soil.

Meat, oil, or dairy products.

What about eucalyptus? There is a common belief that eucalyptus in the pile can inhibit the growth of other plants when the compost is eventually used. A study by the University of California did not find this to be true. It is safe to compost eucalyptus.

inch layers of carbon and nitrogen materials, or toss them all together like stir-fry vegetables in a giant wok. Water the pile as it is being constructed, ensuring that everything is as moist as a damp sponge. It is difficult to moisten the entire pile from the top after it is built. The water quickly finds a channel to run like a river to the bottom of the pile, and most of the organic matter stays dry.

Many gardeners develop their own favorite compost "recipe" as they gain experience. What you put in the pile will depend considerably on the types of waste your yard and kitchen generate or what you can "borrow" from neighbors. They will probably be delighted to hand over their pile of raked leaves or grass clippings.

The size of the pile is important. Backyard compost piles should measure at least one cubic yard (3 feet x 3 feet x 3 feet). This size provides insulation to keep the pile from drying out rapidly, allows air penetration, and is still manageable to turn. You can simply pile the materials into a heap. If you prefer a tidier look, the illustrations feature some easy-to-use compost bins.

Earth-Friendly Gardener

Master Gardener Connie Heaton purchased an electric chipper/shredder to reduce the amount of green waste generated and to recycle it back into her yard. "An electric chipper/shredder is easy to manage and everything under two inches in diameter goes through it," she explains. "Even rose canes, tree and shrub trimmings, sunflower and hollyhock stalks, and tomato vines, which are otherwise difficult to cut up for the compost pile." Connie mixes the shredded matter into her compost pile where it decomposes more quickly because of its reduced size. She spreads the finished compost as mulch around plants and uses it as a soil amendment in her garden.

Carbon and Nitrogen Materials and Ratios

Carbon (Brown) Materials	Carbon : Nitrogen Ratio
Sawdust	200-500 : 1
Woody landscape prunings (branches, stalks, stems)	300 : 1
Shredded newspaper/cardboard	150-200 : 1
Straw	50-80 : 1
Corn stalks	50-60 : 1
Dry leaves	40-80 : 1
Dry hay	40 : 1

Nitrogen (Green) Materials	Carbon : Nitrogen Ratio
Fresh hay	10-25 : 1
Kitchen scraps	15-25 : 1
Leafy trimmings/spent annuals	20-25 : 1
Grass clippings	20-25 : 1
Manures	20-25 : 1
Chicken manure	10 : 1
Coffee grounds/tea bags	15-25 : 1
Weed foliage (no seeds)	20-25 : 1
Hair, fur, feathers	10-25 : 1

Compost Bins

If you have the space, try three bins in a row. The first holds fresh material. After it decomposes for awhile, perhaps one month, toss it into the second bin, remoistening it as you go. Put fresh organic matter into the first bin. When the second bin has decomposed further, another month, move it into the third bin, along with more water to decompose for another month. If you started with small pieces and kept the pile moist, at the end of the month there will be usable compost in the third bin. Toss the first bin into the second, and so on. It is not necessary to use three bins. You can still turn and remoisten material regularly using one bin. Wooden shipping pallets, hardware cloth wire, and cement blocks can be used to make bins. Many cities provide recycled garbage cans that have the bottoms cut off to use for compost bins. They are free or have a nominal charge for residents. Check with your city's waste management department.

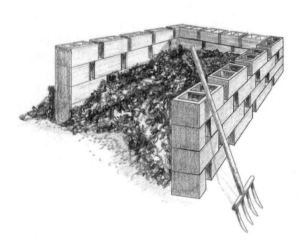

A pitchfork works best to turn the organic matter. Switch to a shovel for finished compost.

When a pile is first constructed, available oxygen is quickly consumed, as are organic materials that are easily decomposed, such as grass clippings. Because of this, the pile will often shrink noticeably in a few days. If you want compost ready in two or three months, turn the pile every week or so, adding more water and nitrogen as needed. The act of turning will incorporate more oxygen.

For best results, the organic matter should always feel like a wrung-out sponge. If you can squeeze water out of it, it is too wet. Overly wet piles are seldom a problem in the Southwest; maintaining sufficient moisture is the challenge. It will help to locate your pile or bin in the shade or cover it with a tarp. Turning and remoistening is important for fast decomposition. If you are not in a hurry, you can construct a good pile and then let it decompose on its own time schedule. It may take 6–24 months for compost to be ready if it is never turned, as long as it is kept moist.

The Decomposition Process

Microorganisms working in a compost pile fall into three broad classes, based on the temperatures at which they thrive. Of course there is overlap in their ranges, but "psychrophiles" live at low temperatures, from about 28 to 70 degrees F. They start the composting process. As the pile heats up, "mesophiles" come on board at around 40 to 70 degrees. They do the bulk of the decomposing, raising the temperature to 100 degrees. At this point, the "thermophiles" take over, boosting the temperature to 140–160 degrees. It is essential that temperatures stay in this hot range for three to five days to kill disease pathogens and weed seeds. As the thermophiles deplete the pile's oxygen and nitrogen, the temperature will gradually drop.

How to Create A "Fast" Pile

The smaller the pieces of organic matter, the speedier the decomposition. Chop material into pieces no larger than two inches in diameter, if possible. Run a lawn mower over leaves to shred them. If you have a lot of landscape waste, consider purchasing a chipper/shredder. A pile turned every three to five days and kept consistently moist will decompose fairly quickly.

Take the pile's temperature regularly. Compost thermometers are about 18 inches long so they can be thrust into the middle of the pile. When it drops below about 110 degrees F, turn the pile. Note that as the pile ages, the temperature will naturally drop as the raw materials decompose into compost.

Bacterial inoculants are sometimes sold to encourage the composting process. However, the surrounding environment and organic materials being composted contain all of the microorganisms needed. It is estimated that one gram of soil contains 100 million bacteria alone. Add a shovelful of native soil to your compost pile for the same benefits.

Retired Mowers

In a period of seven years, Salt River Project utility customers in the Phoenix area retired 14,173 gas-powered lawn mowers and replaced them with earth-friendly electric mowers using SRP's Mowing Down Pollution program. According to the Environmental Protection Agency, replacing those mowers eliminated over 57 tons of summer ozone-causing pollutants and 610 tons of carbon monoxide emissions per year.

Source: SRP

Troubleshooting the Compost Pile

Here are a few issues that sometimes arise with first-time composters.

Nothing seems to be happening. Decomposition is always taking place if moisture is present, even though it may seem unnoticeable. However, the process will slow down if the pile starts to dry, lacks aeration, nitrogen has been used up, or the pile is too small. Turning, remoistening, and adding nitrogen materials will usually jumpstart the process.

There are objectionable odors. A well-constructed pile will not smell. If there is a rotten egg smell, it is too wet. Turn the pile to incorporate more oxygen and/or add carbon materials. If there is an ammonia odor, there is too much nitrogen material, such as a large clump of fresh grass clippings. Because they are so small and full of moisture, grass clippings can mat and rot quickly if they are not well mixed. Turn the pile to aerate and/or add more carbon.

The pile contains grubs, earthworms, or other insects. This is a good thing. These beneficial creatures are decomposing the organic matter. No control is needed. Be glad they are present!

Worm Composting

Vermicomposting (derived from the Latin for worm, *vermis*), is the term used to describe worms as composters. Red wiggler worms are industrious eaters, consuming the equivalent of half their weight in organic matter daily. In other words, two pounds of red wigglers can eat one pound of kitchen scraps.

Not just any garden variety worm is used for vermicomposting. Although all worms are good soil builders, composting worms *(Eisenia fetida* and *Lumbricus rubellus)* process more organic matter faster than earthworms that live deeper in the soil. Composting worms live in nature close to the soil surface where there is a lot of accumulated organic debris, such as rotting leaves and decaying wood. Common names such as red wigglers, red worms, and manure worms are sometimes used interchangeably, but if you buy worms specifically for composting, they're likely to be one of the above two species.

Worm castings (what the worms leave behind after all that eating) are like gold to the avid gardener. The worms have digested and broken down the organic matter into simple forms that are more readily available for uptake by plants. Castings are a rich, dark brown, have a pleasant earthy smell, and somewhat resemble fine coffee grounds.

What's the most important aspect of short-term worm survival? Same as humans in the desert—water. Worm bodies are composed mostly of water and they'll literally dry out without adequate moisture. Some of this they'll obtain from their food, but it's essential that their "bedding" remains moist. Bedding can be any mix of shredded paper, leaves, or soil. Bury the food scraps in the bedding and the worms will find it in no time. Bedding should be completed changed every six months. Just about any type of container can be used as a worm bin, indoors or outside, but keep it out of direct sun.

Earth-Friendly Gardener

Master Composter Carolyn Chard uses red wiggler worms to compost kitchen scraps and other organic matter. Worm castings are high in nutrients, and she suggests adding them to houseplant soil mixes or garden beds, or spreading them on the top of soil as a mulch. The nutrients will seep in with repeated waterings. "I also drain off excess liquid in the worm bin and dilute it with an equal amount of water," says Carolyn. "It makes a nutritious 'tonic' that your potted and bedding plants will love."

Pet Waste

The topic of pet waste may not leap to mind when thinking about landscape maintenance practices that contribute to water pollution. However, pet feces is a major biological contaminant of water runoff. With so many of us sharing our lives with pets, it is essential to dispose of their waste properly.

Like any other pollutant, if pet waste is left on the lawn it can be washed into storm drains, eventually reaching bodies of water. Pet waste contains nutrients, especially nitrogen, that encourage the growth of algae in water. Bacteria and parasites in the waste can spread to humans. Flies that are attracted to the feces may spread diseases.

Do not put pet waste in compost piles as the disease organisms can survive the decomposition process. Do not allow feces to accumulate. Clean up after your pet immediately. Place waste in a securely tied bag in the trash. Take a plastic bag with you when you walk your pet.

Another method is to bury waste in your yard at least five inches deep. It will break down and add nutrients to the soil. To prevent the spread of disease, do not bury near vegetable gardens, wells, children's play areas, or bodies of water.

Fertilizing

All plants require some combination of 17 elements to survive. Nitrogen, phosphorus, and potassium are needed by most plants in fairly large amounts and are called macronutrients. Plants also require other nutrients, such as zinc and manganese, in small amounts, which are called micronutrients. Most fertilizer products are comprised of nitrogen, phosphorus, and potassium in varying amounts. Some fertilizer products contain all of the required elements and are called "complete" fertilizers. Special-purpose fertilizers have a specific combination of nutrients to match the needs of a species, such as rose fertilizer or citrus fertilizer.

Fertilizers can contribute to water pollution and create health risks if misapplied. Nitrogen, in the form of nitrate, is completely soluble and can leach through the soil into groundwater supplies or be carried along with soil particles as runoff into other water sources. Other forms of nitrogen fertilizer, such as ammonium or urea, will eventually be converted to nitrate by soil microorganisms, and thus can also leach through the soil. Phosphorus is relatively immobile in the soil, so it is less likely to leach into the groundwater but can still end up in above-ground water sources. In the low desert, the ground is so hard and dry that very little rainwater can be absorbed before rushing into storm drain systems and eventually reaching rivers, lakes, and wetlands, carrying pollutants along with it.

Why should we be concerned about this? Elevated nitrate levels in drinking water reduce the blood's ability to transport oxygen, especially in infants. Too much phosphate in a body of water leads to a burgeoning algae and weed population that eventually out-competes other plants and fish, altering its basic ecosystem.

Pollutants reach our water supplies in a myriad of ways. "Point source pollution" is generated from a single, specific location, such as a factory. It is relatively easy to determine the origin and develop controls. "Non-point source pollution" is not easy to trace to its origin. This pollution comes from many sources, which makes it difficult to control. Homeowners unknowingly add to non-point source pollution from well-intentioned but inappropriate landscaping practices. Although one household may not contribute much to the problem, millions of homeowners combined add a significant slice to the pollution pie. Pollutants become concentrated on lawns, driveways, and streets and eventually wash into waterways during rain showers or leach through the soil to groundwater sources. On the positive side, we can easily reduce non-source point pollution by applying fertilizer correctly and only if needed. Pesticides are another component of non-point source pollution and their use will be covered in the next chapter.

Do Your Plants Need Fertilizer?

Sometimes plants can not obtain all the nutrients they need from the surrounding soil for a variety of reasons. The soil may be lacking some elements. Desert soils are typically low in organic matter, which results in low nitrogen levels. Desert plants have adapted to this condition either by requiring less nitrogen or making their own. For example, cacti don't need much nitrogen to remain healthy. Most desert trees, such as mesquite, acacia, palo verde, and ironwood, are in the legume family. Legumes, in a mutually beneficial relationship with certain soil bacteria, have the ability to create usable nitrogen by converting atmospheric nitrogen into ammonia, and then ammonia into nitrate. Nitrate can be readily absorbed by root systems, whereas the other two forms of nitrogen cannot. If landscape plants are native to regions with organic soil high in nitrogen, they will most likely struggle in desert soil and require fertilization.

Another possibility is that the nutrients exist in the soil, but a plant can not uptake them. Roots require a complicated balance of soil moisture, temperature, and pH to absorb available nutrients and transport them through the plant. (pH is a measure of acidity/alkalinity.) In order for plants to pull in nutrients through their roots, the nutrients must be dissolved in water in the soil. If the soil is too dry or even too wet, the plant can't absorb the nutrients. Every species has its own preferred conditions, and if these conditions are not met, applying fertilizer will not help. For example, if soil is too wet or too dry for extended periods, plant foliage may yellow. Adjusting how the plant is watered—increasing or decreasing the frequency and ensuring the water reaches the entire root system—addresses the problem. Applying fertilizer, a common reaction when yellow leaves appear, does not.

It is unnecessary to regularly apply fertilizer to all plants as part of a scheduled maintenance routine. Most established desert plants do not need fertilizer. Some plants, such as citrus, turfgrasses, and roses, do require a regular fertilizing program to maintain optimum health. Other healthy landscape plants may benefit from just one feeding as they come out of dormancy in the spring.

Use the following information to help determine which plant categories may require supplemental nutrition. Eliminate unnecessary fertilizer applications and save it for plants that do need it.

Native or desert-adapted landscape plants, cacti, and succulents. They seldom require fertilizer as they have adapted to thrive with the existing soil. Nutrient deficiencies are rare. Select natives to avoid the expense and time required to fertilize.

Non-adapted landscape plants. These plants usually need nitrogen fertilizer.

Newly planted trees or shrubs. Do not apply fertilizer for at least one year after planting. This is a change in planting guidelines from years ago, when fertilizer was often mixed into the planting hole or applied a couple weeks after transplanting. Fertilizer encourages the young plant to put on new growth, when it would be better off expending its energy on developing its root system. Plants that grow too fast are stressed, becoming more susceptible to pests and diseases. Overfertilized plants also require more frequent watering and pruning.

Vegetable and flower beds. Annual plants exert a lot of energy to grow, flower, set fruit, and reproduce all in one season, so they need nutrient-rich soil. Adding organic matter, such as compost or well-rotted manure, to the beds before each growing season will enhance soil fertility and provide variable amounts of nutrients, depending on the source of the material. Incorporate nitrogen and phosphorus fertilizer into the soil before planting and apply nitrogen about four to five weeks into the growing season. Heavy nitrogen users such as leafy greens, corn, and cabbage family crops (broccoli, cauliflower, Brussels sprouts) may need additional fertilizer every few weeks depending on your soil's fertility. Flowers and fruiting crops (tomatoes, squash, peppers) do not. Excess nitrogen will promote foliage growth at the expense of the flowers and fruit and may be leached into groundwater supplies.

Wildflowers. They are well-adapted to desert soil and do not typically need fertilizer.

Palms. Yellowing in palms, queen palms in particular, is usually caused by a lack of nitrogen, or perhaps potassium, manganese, or magnesium. Use a fertilizer formulated for palms, which will have an appropriate mix of nutrients. Do not fertilize newly planted palms. Wait until the next growing season to apply fertilizer. Established palms need feeding only once or twice per year, during their active growing season. Apply fertilizer in mid spring and/or early summer.

Roses, turf, citrus, fruit, and nut trees. These plants need fertilizer to thrive. There are publications listed in the Resources that contain specific recommendations for fertilizing these plants, including types of fertilizer, amount, and frequency. Most County Cooperative Extension offices will have fertilizer guidelines for their specific region.

Container plants. Potted plants quickly deplete available nutrients and roots can't expand past the confines of the container to seek more. Nutrients are washed away by the frequent waterings that most containers require. Containers with leafy foliage or flowering plants need fertilizer, perhaps as often as every two weeks. Slow-release fertilizers in containers reduce this frequency. Potted cacti and other succulents need small amounts of fertilizer monthly, but only during their growing season.

Diagnosing Nutrient Deficiencies

Regularly examine all of your plants for signs of nutrient deficiency. Nitrogen and iron are the elements most commonly lacking in desert soil. Phosphorus, potassium, or micronutrient deficiencies seldom occur.

Nitrogen

As stated earlier, desert soil has a low-nitrogen content. Nitrogen fertilizer is highly soluble so it is used up quickly or leached or washed away during heavy rain or frequent irrigation. Most non-desert foliage plants require additional nitrogen. These three factors combine to make nitrogen the element most commonly lacking in the desert landscape or garden.

Nitrogen deficiency appears as yellowing on older, lower leaves. If the condition becomes more severe, new leaves may also be yellow. Nitrogen deficiency is corrected with fertilizer, as opposed to cultural adjustments in plant care. If you grow plants that require considerable nitrogen, such as citrus, fertilize them on a regular schedule to prevent deficiency, which is stressful to plants.

Deficiencies in nitrogen and iron both show up as yellow leaves—a condition called chlorosis. Although they may appear similar at first glance, you can tell the difference by examining the leaves.

Iron

Iron deficiency appears as yellow leaves with green veins. It strikes new leaves first, then moves to older leaves. Our desert soils are alkaline, in the range of 8.0 to 8.5 on the pH scale. Although there is usually sufficient iron present, it is not readily soluble in alkaline soil making it unavailable for non-desert plants to uptake. In addition, iron is less available in cold, wet soils or extremely dry soils. Symptoms of iron deficiency may appear during rainy winters or on overwatered plants with roots sitting in wet soil.

Because iron deficiency may be caused by weather and soil conditions, the chlorosis may correct itself when the temperature changes or watering schedules are changed. If there is no improvement after these adjustments, apply a chelated iron source. Chelates hold the iron in solution so that it is readily available for uptake by roots for a longer period of time than non-chelated iron sources.

Phosphorus

Phosphorus deficiencies are rare but it is beneficial to put a phosphorus fertilizer at the bottom of the planting hole for flowering and fruiting annual plants to make it available to the root systems. Applying it to the soil surface does little good, as phosphorus does not move readily through soil. Because of its immobility, place phosphorus where the roots are, or where they are going to grow.

Organic gardeners in the low desert have limited choices for phos-

(l) Nitrogen deficiency appears as yellowing on older leaves, usually lower on the plant.

(r) Iron deficiency appears as yellow leaves with green veins, starting on new leaves.

phorus, an important element for flowering and fruiting plants. Bone meal has traditionally been recommended for organic gardening, but it is largely ineffective according to Thomas Thompson, Associate Soil Specialist with the University of Arizona Cooperative Extension. "Bone meal is comprised of calcium phosphates, which are highly insoluble in all soils, and especially so in alkaline soils," he explains. "Thus, it would take a long time for any significant phosphorus to be in a form that plants could use." An additional factor is how the bone meal is created. "The processing and extraction system is more intense than it used to be," states Thompson, "resulting in less available phosphorus." Rock phosphate, the other organic source typically recommended, is also highly insoluble in alkaline soils. Compost and manures contain some phosphorus but the concentration is low and highly variable depending on the source and age of the organic matter.

Understanding Fertilizer Products

There is an abundant selection of fertilizer products on the shelves of garden supply stores. The following information will help you understand some of the characteristics so you can choose the product best suited for your needs.

NPK

Fertilizer containers must be labeled with the percentages of their contents by weight. The three numbers prominently displayed are called the NPK ratio, representing nitrogen (N), phosphorus (P), and potassium (K). For example, a 15-30-15 fertilizer contains 15 percent nitrogen, 30 percent phosphate, and 15 percent potassium. It is called a "complete" fertilizer because it contains these three important elements. Manufacturers are required by law to guarantee the percentages are accurate. In general terms, nitrogen maintains green, healthy foliage; phosphorus strengthens roots and stems and produces flowers and fruits; and potassium is associated with disease resistance, internal structures, and cycling the plant into dormancy.

Most desert soils contain plenty of potassium, so this nutrient does not need to be included when fertilizing. (If you have a fertilizer product that contains potassium it doesn't hurt to apply it.) An exception is Bermudagrass. If you regularly use a fertilizer that contains only nitrogen, a fall application of potassium helps the turf go into dormancy and come out of dormancy in spring with more strength and vigor. Apply one-half pound of potassium per 1000 square feet. If you normally use a lawn fertilizer that contains potassium, this extra application is not necessary.

Organic or Inorganic

Organic fertilizers are made from the decomposed remains of once-living things. Inorganic fertilizers are made from mineral salts. From the plant's point of view, there is no difference between the nutrients provided by the two. "At that submicroscopic root hair and nutrient interface, root systems take up nutrients in the same elemental form whether they originated from organic or inorganic sources," explains Terry Mikel, University of Arizona Cooperative Extension Commercial Horticulture Agent. However, organic fertilizers provide benefits for an earth-friendly landscape that inorganics do not. Because they are adding organic matter to the soil, even in small quantities, they help improve soil fertility and structure over time. They encourage the activity of beneficial soil organisms and earthworms, which are industrious soil builders. Organics are slow to break down in the soil, so they are less likely to be washed or leached away to contaminate water sources. Conversely, they must break down further before the nutrients can be absorbed, thus they act more slowly on plants. Organic fertilizers are more expensive than inorganics and their NPK ratio is usually low, such as 5-3-1.

Inorganic fertilizers are more likely to contribute to pollution because they are readily soluble and can leach through the soil or wash away, especially if overapplied. They are fast-acting on plants but can also burn roots if used inappropriately. Inorganics do not improve or help build the soil. The salts they are made of can accumulate in the soil over time and cause salt burn if plants are not watered deeply to leach salts beyond the root zone. Salt burn appears as yellowing and browning on the edges of the leaves. However, if plants show signs of nutrient deficiency, an inorganic product will act more rapidly on the problem than an organic one.

Fertilizer/Pesticide Combinations

As a general rule, it is unnecessary to use fertilizers that also contain pesticides in the home landscape. It is quite difficult to predict that a plant will need fertilizer at the same time it needs protection from pest attack.

Granular

Granular fertilizer is most effective if applied in conjunction with a regular irrigation. Before fertilizing, apply the first half of a normal irrigation, fertilize, then apply the second half of the irrigation. Nitrogen-only fertilizer does not need to be scratched into the soil surface because nitrogen is so soluble it will soak in readily. However, because it is so soluble, do not leave it on the soil surface or apply it to saturated soil, as some of the nitrogen will be lost. If using a complete fertilizer, it helps to scratch it into the soil. Another method is to mix granular fertilizer with water in a bucket and pour it immediately into the plant's watering well. Note that fertilizers should be applied so that irrigation water can move nutrients into the soil. Thus, the pattern of fertilizer application should differ depending on the type of irrigation system used.

Liquid

Liquid fertilizers help ensure an even distribution. The product, in either powder, pellet, or liquid form, is diluted in water according to package instructions and then poured on the root zone. It works well if plants have watering wells that allow it to soak in.

Slow-Release

Slow-release fertilizers release their nutrients over a period of time, usually three to six months. Plants benefit with a more steady supply of

Earth-Friendly Gardener

Master Gardener Copper Bittner demonstrates how enacting just one earth-friendly practice serves multiple purposes in the landscape. Her homeowner's association mandates a year-round green lawn, so she started a compost pile for the grass clippings. She adds all of her food scraps (except meat and dairy) and even shredded paper from her office, thereby reducing further the amount of waste sent to the landfill each week. "The compost pile is located behind my orange tree and when I soak the tree, it receives compost tea as an organic fertilizer," explains Copper. "I use the compost as a mulch around all my other plants to cut down on evaporation and keep their roots cooler." Since starting this cycle in her yard, Copper has cut water usage by one-third and eliminated all other fertilizer applications.

nutrients. Slow-release products have been coated with a substance that, when in contact with moist soil, releases some of the nutrient. Slow-release products are usually more expensive but do not have to be applied as frequently. They work well for containers or small garden areas.

Foliar

Foliar spray applications are a useful method to get nutrients into a plant's system quickly. The fertilizer is sprayed directly on the plant tissue, which begins absorbing it within minutes. The nutrients are usually absorbed within one or two days. Care must be taken so that leaf tissue is not burned. Apply early in the morning before the sun heats up. Test a few leaves first and wait a day before spraying the entire plant. Foliar feeding should not be used exclusively in lieu of good soil nutrition. It is a useful method to correct a micronutrient deficiency or when cold soil limits the nutrients available for uptake. Be careful if you use this method, as overspraying can stain sidewalks and decks.

Injectors

The practice of injecting fertilizers below the soil surface is not recommended, for several reasons. First, this is unnecessary with soluble fertilizers, which will be moved into the soil with proper irrigation and application procedures. Second, injection can actually cause the nutrients to bypass the feeder roots near the soil surface, the most important part of the root zone for nutrient uptake. Finally, injection can create areas of high salt concentration within the root zone, which can harm the roots.

Earth-Friendly Gardener

Master Gardener Linda Trujillo improves the nutrient level in her garden beds by rotating crops with legumes, which help "fix" nitrogen in the soil. "I had trouble enriching carrot beds with composted manures and other standard nitrogen fertilizers," she says. "Too much nitrogen increased the foliage and decreased the size and quality of the carrot." Her solution was to rotate the cool-season crops, like carrots, with warm-season legumes, such as lima beans. This allowed her to reduce her fertilizer application by 50 percent, as she now adds organic matter and fertilizer once per year, rather than twice.

Apply fertilizer and water at and slightly beyond a plant's dripline where "feeder" roots are able to uptake it.

Where and When to Apply Fertilizer

All fertilizers, even organic, can end up in the water supply if inappropriately applied. It sounds like common sense, but always follow the package instructions for application rates. The theory that "a scoop of ice cream is good, and two scoops is much better" does not apply to fertilizers. Overfertilizing stresses a plant, making it vulnerable to pest and disease attack. It can even result in root burn and death of the plant. Before the plant can use that extra fertilizer, it will leach through the soil to contaminate groundwater or wash away, eventually ending up in streams, lakes, and riparian habitats.

Apply fertilizers at and slightly beyond a plant's dripline—the outer edge of its canopy. This is where its roots are actively taking up water and nutrients.

Different plant species have varying needs for fertilizer at different times of the year. (See the accompanying chart for guidelines.) For most landscape plants, fertilizer is usually applied just before plants come out of winter dormancy and actively begin growing in early spring. In the low desert, that's late January–February. At higher elevations, apply after your last average annual frost date. Check with a local nursery, other gardeners, or the County Cooperative Extension office for the date in your area. Few plants need fertilizer in the heat of summer in the low desert. This a stressful period for most plants and forcing them to grow is cruel and unusual punishment. An exception is palm trees and lawns, which are actively growing in summer. Some plants may benefit from a light application of fertilizer in early fall to help them with their second growth spurt that occurs as summer's heat abates. Do not apply fertilizer to landscape plants in late fall. Fertilizing stimulates tender new growth, which is susceptible to frost damage. Fertilizer applied during dormant winter months is wasted as roots can not uptake nutrients in cold, wet soil.

When to Fertilize Plants in the Low Desert												
	Jan	Feb	Mar	Apr	May	Jun	Jul	Aug	Sep	Oct	Nov	Dec
Non-desert landscape	X *or*	X							X			
Roses	X	X	X	X					X	X		
Citrus	X *or*	X		X *or*	X			X *or*	X			
Fruit trees		X										
Nut trees		X										
Palms			X	*and/or*	X							
Ryegrass	X	X	X	X	X							X
Bermuda				X	X	X	X	X	X	X		

Pruning

As discussed in Chapter 3, it is best to choose a plant that will grow only as large as its allotted space in the landscape rather than cutting it back because it gets too tall or wide. Plants have a better chance to stay healthy if they undergo fewer pruning cuts, which are basically open wounds for pests and diseases to gain easy entry. Of course the less you prune, the less green waste you generate, which has to be either recycled into the landscape or sent to a landfill. Frequent pruning eliminates the colorful appeal of flowers, berries, and seeds, all of which attract birds to the landscape. If you are frequently pruning a plant to prevent it from scratching people as they walk by, or to limit its height because of overhead obstructions, consider replacing it with a plant whose size fits that location. You will save considerable time and expense in the long run.

Valid reasons for pruning include removing dead, diseased, damaged, weak, or crossed limbs, both for the plant's health and to eliminate potential safety hazards. If you decide some trimming is justified, learn how to make proper pruning cuts for a more attractive appearance and to maintain the long-term health of the plant. Do not remove more than 25 percent of any plant in one year.

Make a Good Pruning Cut

Trees and shrubs have a special tissue that helps them to heal after a branch is broken or a pruning cut is made. It is called meristematic tissue and it is located in the angle where smaller branches meet larger branches. Meristematic tissue grows relatively quickly and seals the opening. Your goal when pruning is to leave this tissue intact so it can do its job. It was once a common practice to cover pruning cuts with various paints or sealants, but experts no longer recommend this. It interferes with the meristematic tissue's functioning and may seal in harmful bacteria.

With a little practice, you can learn to recognize where the meristematic tissue is located and make a proper pruning cut. (See illustration on next page.) The "branch bark ridge" is a raised furrow of bark on the top of a branch, found in the angle between the branch and its adjoining trunk. The "branch collar" is a raised furrow of bark on the underside of the branch where it meets the trunk. The meristematic tissue resides in this collar. A good pruning cut makes a direct line connecting the branch bark ridge and the branch collar, thus leaving the meristematic tissue untouched.

How to Prune Large, Heavy Limbs

If not removed properly, the weight of large limbs can rip the bark down the tree's trunk when cut, leaving an unsightly and unhealthy wound. Follow this simple three-step procedure to eliminate this problem.

First, make an undercut (cut upward from bottom) one-quarter of the way through the branch, about 6–12 inches beyond the final cut location. This first cut will stop the bark from tearing.

Arizona Community Tree Council

A non-profit organization that promotes communication and the exchange of information about trees, and the essential role they play in the well-being of all Arizona communities. ACTC encourages and facilitates the planting and care of trees throughout the state. Their website contains links to many tree-related sites. 1616 W. Adams, Phoenix, AZ 85007, 602-542-6191. http://aztrees.org/.

Second, make a top cut (top down) slightly beyond the first cut, sawing the branch completely off. This eliminates most of the weight, making it easier to remove the remainder without damaging the trunk.

Third, make a pruning cut as described earlier, sawing a direct line connecting the branch bark ridge and the branch collar, leaving the meristematic tissue to heal the wound.

When to Prune

The best time to prune shrubs depends upon their bloom period. Spring-blooming shrubs should be pruned after they finish flowering. Summer-blooming shrubs are best pruned during their winter dormancy, usually January. Non-native deciduous trees and conifers are also pruned when they are winter dormant. Prune native trees in May or early June, as they are beginning their active growth period in summer and it will speed their recovery.

Pruning Tools

Choose by-pass pruners and by-pass loppers rather than anvil pruners or loppers. By-pass tools have a scissors action and make a clean cut that can heal properly. Anvil tools direct the blade against a flat surface that crushes plant tissue as it cuts. For branches larger than 1.5 inches in diameter, use a razor tooth pruning saw. Avoid hedge trimmers and hedge shears, which cut all branches at the same length, not allowing selective pruning for a natural shape.

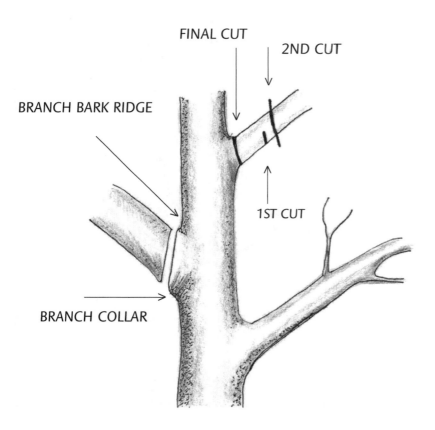

FINAL CUT

2ND CUT

BRANCH BARK RIDGE

1ST CUT

BRANCH COLLAR

A good pruning cut is a direct line connecting the branch bark ridge and branch collar, which allows the tree's natural healing mechanisms to seal the wound. On large heavy limbs, make three cuts to prevent bark from tearing down the side of the trunk.

Beneficial Insects

(l) Minute pirate bug

(r) Praying mantid adult

(l) Praying mantid egg case

(r) Sun spider

(l) Crab spider

(r) Black widow spider catches a cockroach in its nest

(l) Whipscorpion

(r) Tailless whipscorpion

(below, l to r) Ladybeetle pupae, larva feeding on aphid, adult feeding on aphid

Insects

Beneficial Insects

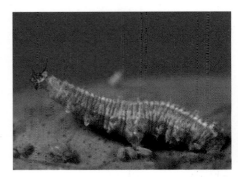

(l) Syrphid fly adult

(r) Syrphid fly larva feeding on aphids

(l) Syrphid fly adult close-up

(r) *Trichogramma* wasp laying an egg in a corn earworm egg

(l) Parasitic wasp laying egg

(r) Parasitic wasp laying its egg in an armyworm

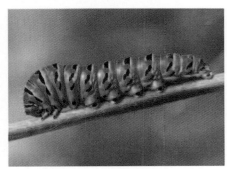

(l) Swallowtail larva

(r) Swallowtail adult

(below, l to r) Gulf fritillary adult, larva, adult

83

Beneficial Insects

(l) Monarch larva

(r) Monarch pupa

Bees and butterflies are excellent pollinators. Enjoy their presence in your yard!

(l) Monarch adult

(r) Bumble bee

(l) Swallowtail adult

(r) Honey bee

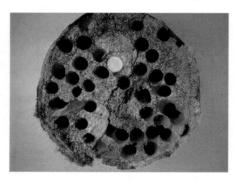

(l) Carpenter bee "nests"

Cool-Season Insects

(r) Beet leafhopper

(below, l to r) Aphid adults aphid mummies (magnified), adults

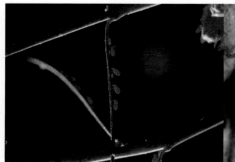

Cool-Season Insects

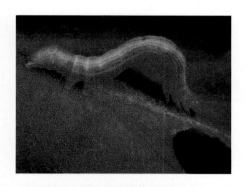

(l) Cabbage looper, easily recognized by the "loop" it makes when crawling

(r) Cabbage looper adult

(l) Cabbage looper damage

(r) Thrip on base of flower petal

(l) Onion thrips

(r) Thrip scarring to citrus peel is cosmetic only and does not influence fruit quality

Warm-Season Insects

(l) Agave weevil

(r) Agave collapse from weevil damage

(l) Cicada adult

(r) Cicada exoskeleton

<u>Warm-Season Insects</u>

(l) Cochineal scale

(r) Cochineal scale

(l) False chinch bugs on grape cane

(r) False chinch bugs clustering on rock

(l) Green June beetle

(r) Fig beetle

(l) June beetle larvae

(r) Fig beetle larvae

(below) Cutworm with seedling damage, adult, cutworm damage to potatoes

Insects

Warm-Season Insects

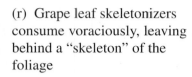

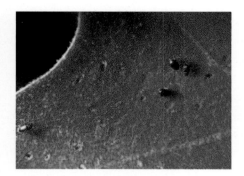

(l) Flea beetles

(r) Grape leaf skeletonizers consume voraciously, leaving behind a "skeleton" of the foliage

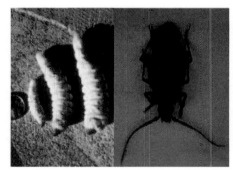

(l) Palm flower caterpillars

(r) Palo verde root borer grubs and adult (coin as size comparison)

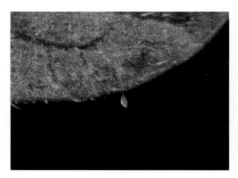

(l) Psyllid adult

(r) Psyllid egg and nymph

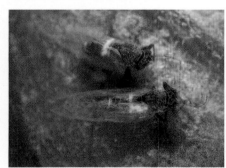

(l) Psyllid adults

(r) Psyllid damage

(bottom, l to r) Leafcutter bee, half-moon cuts by bees in foliage, leafcutter nests made of foliage

87

Warm-Season Insects

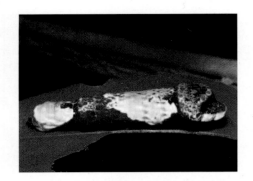

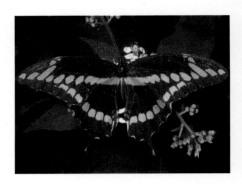

(l) Orange dog caterpillar (giant swallowtail larva)

(r) Giant swallowtail

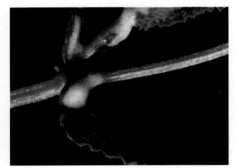

(l) Spittle bug

(r) Salt marsh caterpillar (migrating caterpillar)

(l) Mites in a cluster (rusty color)

(r) Spider mite damage on melon foliage

(l) White-lined sphinx moth is one species of hornworm adult

(r) Tobacco hornworm

(l) Whitefly adults and immatures (magnified)

(r) Whiteflies on foliage undersides

Chapter 5

Integrated Pest Management

The concept of "pest" can be defined in a variety of ways, but for our purposes it is a creature or disease that is causing more damage to plants than we can tolerate. Weeds can also be considered as pests if they are providing food and shelter for insect pests or competing with desirable plants for nutrients and water. Integrated Pest Management (IPM) is a somewhat fancy term for a common-sense system that helps us decide if pests need to be controlled and, if so, what combination of control methods will be the most earth-friendly and cost-effective. IPM is being used successfully in a wide range of situations, including homes, schools, and large-scale agriculture. For example, an IPM pilot program conducted by University of Arizona entomologists at a Tempe-area school district reduced pesticide use by 90 percent and the total number of pests by an estimated 85 percent. (See the Resources for the *IPM in Schools* website that describes the program in detail.)

Why Use IPM?

The basic principles of Integrated Pest Management were proposed in the 1970s as an alternative to synthetic pesticides such as DDT or 2,4D. (A pesticide is any substance designed to kill insects, fungi, weeds, rodents, or any other pest.) Developed during World War II, these synthetics were more powerful than other options for pest control. Any associated problems that may have arisen with their use were considered minimal. In the following two decades, synthetic pesticides became the treatment of choice and were often sprayed as a preventive measure on a regular schedule whether or not pests were causing significant damage. This sole reliance on pesticides, without considering the health of the entire ecosystem, began to backfire. Problems emerged such as resistance, resurgence, secondary pest outbreaks, and harmful residue.

Resistance. The concept of "survival of the fittest" began to appear all too frequently. Individual pests that had resistance to any particular pesticide survived to reproduce offspring who were also resistant. Genetic selection produced hundreds of species, including cockroaches and mosquitoes, that are now resistant to a range of pesticides.

Resurgence. Many of the synthetic pesticides were indiscriminate, meaning they killed all insects, including those that were natural enemies of the pest. With nothing to consume them, the pest population came back in greater numbers than existed before spraying took place.

Secondary Pest Outbreaks. Other potential pests are not problems until their natural enemies are killed by spraying. With their normal biological control method wiped out, a new pest problem arises. This outcome was observed in California fruit orchards. Farmers were spraying to control cottony cushion scale. Suddenly the numbers of spider mites, another pest, increased dramatically because the various natural enemies that kept the mites in check had also been killed by spraying for the scale.

Residue. The remains of pesticides stay in the environment and create direct health problems for wildlife and humans who are exposed to them. Pesticides can also cause indirect consequences that are harder to predict. For example, toxic effects become more concentrated as a substance moves up the food chain in a process called "biomagnification." Another consequence is "synergism," in which toxic effects increase when a pesticide is exposed to other environmental factors or other chemicals.

Principles of IPM

IPM seeks to eliminate these types of problems associated with a sole reliance on synthetic pesticides. It takes into consideration all possible methods of control to create an overall strategy, preferably using synthetics only as a last resort. A plant's health and ability to tolerate some damage, as well as natural enemies of the pest, are important factors. The goal of IPM is to solve a problem with the least toxic effects to humans, the environment, and other living creatures. An IPM program follows these steps:

❏ Prevent problems with good plant care
❏ Identify insects that are present
❏ Monitor the situation for numbers of insects and amount of plant damage
❏ Decide if control is required
❏ Choose control methods, starting with the least-toxic method
❏ Keep records and evaluate results

Prevent Problems with Good Plant Care

As discussed in Chapter 4, proper plant maintenance is the first step in preventing problems. IPM encourages vigilance to spot any insect activity or signs of stress and disease. When a plant is stressed, insects and diseases take advantage of its weakened state. Often their arrival can be considered a by-product of an underlying adverse condition. Rather than treating the surface pest, you may need to identify and correct a problem with the plant's environment or how you maintain it, such as insufficient light or overwatering.

Identify Any Insects

If you see an unfamiliar insect, identify it before taking action. Many of us are conditioned by years of advertising to reach for a spray can the moment we spot any bug. Many insects are beneficial and some pests should be tolerated if they are not doing extensive damage. It is estimated that only one to five percent of insects have the potential to be pests. You might see an insect in a stage of development with which you are unfamiliar. For example, most people can identify ladybeetles, but do you know what the larvae look like? They are as voracious, if not more so, than the adult and can consume up to 400 aphids during their lifetime. Another factor to consider is that some insects that we consider to be pests are an essential part of the ecosystem. For example, termites are a problem if they are reducing homes to sawdust, but their ability to recycle organic

---

Plants Become Stressed If They Are:

✓ Overwatered.

✓ Underwatered.

✓ Planted in a location that does not fulfill their cultural needs for sunlight, temperature, and soil type.

✓ Not adapted to the region. Native plants are adapted to withstand local conditions, which includes local insects and diseases.

✓ Forced to grow too fast by overfertilizing. Tender new growth is susceptible to attack from pests.

✓ Unable to obtain specific nutrients.

matter is essential to the cycle of life. Therefore, as we protect our homes from termite activity, we should not try to eliminate all termites from the environment.

Monitor The Situation

Watch for a few days to see what changes take place. Jot down notes to help you keep track. Is there an increase in the number of pests? Insects often go away with changes in temperature or they are eaten by other insects, spiders, birds, centipedes, and lizards, thus providing an important link in the food chain.

Decide If Control Is Required

It isn't necessary, or even a good idea, to try to eliminate every insect to have healthy plants. No intervention is the most earth-friendly method. Determine if the insect is causing sufficient damage to justify managing or controlling it. Are there just a few holes in the foliage, or is the entire plant decimated? Is the damage cosmetic only, or is it threatening the plant's health? Most healthy plants will withstand some moderate damage. Beneficial insects may arrive to consume pests. Seasonal changes in temperature may influence a pest's ability to thrive and reproduce. For example, whiteflies die back when colder temperatures arrive. Aphids, on the other hand, are cool-season pests and disappear when temperatures warm. If the numbers don't grow too large or damage remains minimal or cosmetic, no action may be needed.

Choose Control Methods

If you decide some type of control is required, start with the least-toxic method for that pest. Many options will be described below, most of which are quite simple and do not introduce potentially harmful substances into our homes or landscapes. "Integrating" all possible methods, with the least disruption to nature's ability to achieve a balance, is the basis of Integrated Pest Management. This ultimately reduces our reliance on synthetic pesticides. Call your County Cooperative Extension office for alternatives if you are not sure what methods suit your situation.

Keep Records and Evaluate Results

Take a few moments to record what is happening in your landscape. A garden journal detailing when insects appeared in your landscape and what effect they had on plants is a useful resource. Most insect populations are seasonal so you can be on the lookout for their arrival next year, ready to take needed action or to be aware that the problem will resolve itself. Make specific notes about any control methods you tried and how effective they were.

Types of IPM Control Methods

With time, most gardeners who practice IPM find they don't need to use pesticides. Eliminating their use allows a diverse and valuable popu-

Earth-Friendly Gardener

Desert Botanical Garden Horticulturist and Master Gardener Kirti Mathura, co-author of *Desert Landscaping for Beginners*, recalls one cool season a few years ago when aphids were particularly bad. She sprayed her plants with soapy water for a week or two, but then got busy with other things and stopped the spraying. "Within a few days, I had three species of warblers and a green-tailed towhee in my yard and these birds had eliminated the aphids," she says. "Be patient or lazy and nature will take care of itself," she laughingly recommends.

lation of insects to create their own ecosystem in the landscape. Nature strikes its own balance and in doing so, provides an amazing example of its diversity, complexity, and resiliency. The following information provides a variety of ways to manage pest populations without using synthetic pesticides, including cultural, mechanical, physical, and biological methods.

Cultural Controls

Cultural methods involve maintaining healthy plants using the earth-friendly techniques described in this book and making adjustments in plant care if signs of stress appear. Some examples of cultural methods include:

❑ Water deeply to reduce salt build-up in the root zone.

❑ Increase the time between watering so roots don't sit in overly wet soil.

❑ Water the soil, not the plant. Wet foliage promotes fungal diseases.

❑ Spread mulch to maintain consistent soil moisture.

❑ Pull weeds as soon as they appear as they are easier to pull when young. They compete vigorously for water and nutrients and harbor pests if allowed to grow.

❑ Prune dead or diseased branches. Do not paint the cut with sealant, which interferes with the tree's natural healing ability. (Roses are the only plant benefiting from sealed pruning cuts, which prevents cane borers from entering the open tissue.)

❑ Rotate the location where vegetable crops or annual flowers are planted each season to prevent the build-up of crop-specific pests.

❑ Plant disease-resistant varieties. Disease-resistant seeds have letters at the end of their names on seed packets or may be described in nursery catalogs. For example, 'Celebrity' VFNT on a tomato seed packet means that the 'Celebrity' variety is resistant to Verticillium, Fusarium, Nematodes, and Tobacco Mosaic, all diseases that can devastate tomato plants. A catalog description for Zinnia elegans 'Oklahoma' states "less susceptible to powdery mildew," a fungal disease that strikes many zinnias.

❑ Allow sufficient space between plants for air circulation and sun exposure, which helps prevent powdery mildew.

❑ Clean up plant debris and put in the compost pile. Dispose of anything with pest or disease problems in the trash.

Mechanical and Physical Controls

Mechanical and physical methods either inhibit insects from getting on your plants or remove them if they do. For example:

Soapy Water Recipe

Use 1 teaspoon to no more than 2 tablespoons of liquid detergent soap per gallon of water. Use regular, not concentrated soap. Don't use soaps with lemon, as the citric acid can burn plants. Start with the lower amount and work up if needed. Test it on a few leaves first before you treat all your plants. Spray early in the morning when foliage is cool and can dry before the heat of the day. Never spray plants during the heat of the day.

❑ Erect barriers, such as cardboard collars around the stem of vegetable plants to deter cutworms or floating row cover (white, lightweight material usually made from polypropylene) over tomatoes to discourage leafhoppers from landing.

❑ Handpick large insects. Wear gloves as some insects sting or bite.

❑ Place traps, such as sunken plastic containers with beer or a mix of sugar water and yeast, to attract slugs. They fall in and drown.

❑ Remove entire leaves if heavily infested.

❑ Wash off insects or mites with a spray of water from the hose. If this proves to be ineffective, use a soapy water spray. Soap is slightly more aggressive than plain water. (Although a detergent solution is less toxic than a synthetic pesticide, it is technically classified as a chemical control.)

Biological Controls

Biological controls include predators, parasites, or pathogens that are natural enemies of pests. Predators attack and consume their prey, sometimes by piercing them with sharp mouthparts and sucking out their body juices. Predators include ladybeetles, praying mantids, green lacewings, and spiders, as well as insect-eating birds, lizards, frogs, toads, and bats.

Parasites obtain their food from another organism, referred to as a host, over a period of time. Often parasites lay eggs on the host, or insert the eggs within its body. When the eggs hatch, they feed on the host, eventually killing it.

Pathogens, such as bacteria, fungi, and viruses, cause disease in another organism. *Bacillus thuringiensis* (Bt) is a bacteria that disrupts the digestive system of caterpillars. *Bacillus thurengiensis* var. *israelensis* is used in ponds to control mosquito larvae.

Some biological controls, especially parasites, are highly specialized, preying on only one or two species; others are indiscriminate and consume a wide range of insects, good and bad. Even though you may not notice them, predators that eat many species are most likely at work in your landscape right now as there is always something for them to consume. Some examples of biological controls follow and photographs are in the color section of the book.

Almost all birds eat insects at some point in their lives. Attract birds to your landscape as a method of biological pest control.

Beneficial Biological Controls

Assassin bugs. These bugs have a long, narrow head, body, and legs as well as impressively long antennae. Assassin bugs are about one-half inch long and one-quarter inch wide. Some species have attractive reddish or brownish markings. They have spiny or sticky legs to help them trap prey. They suck juices from their prey using a long, thin beak or tube for a mouth. Adults lay clusters of brown eggs.

Big-eyed bugs. Aptly named for the oversized eyes that seem to protrude from the sides of the head, these grayish-brownish bugs are one-eighth inch long and wide. Nymphs look similar but lack wings. Both adults and nymphs are predators. Single white eggs are identified by a red spot that appears shortly after they are laid.

Centipedes. Nocturnal predators, centipedes are recognized by flat body segments, each with a pair of legs, although not the hundred legs for which they are named. The most common species in the low desert averages three inches long and is tan colored, like desert soil. Centipedes hide during the day under rocks and will scramble for cover if exposed to sunlight. They eat a variety of insects and spiders.

Damsel bugs. They have long narrow bodies shaped somewhat like assassin bugs, including long antennae, but damsels are not as large and lack the interesting coloration. Damsel bugs are three-eighths inch long in shades of brown. Nymphs look similar but lack wings. Both adults and nymphs consume prey.

Green lacewing larvae. One of the prettiest and most effective predators to visit your garden, pale green lacewing adults have delicately veined wings and golden eyes. They typically don't consume pests, feeding mostly on nectar. Adults lay a single white egg at the end of a thin "thread" that is one-quarter to one-half inch long. This method keeps the hatching larvae from being close enough to consume each other. Green lacewing larvae are one of the most voracious predator insects, eating 200 aphids per week, as well as larger insects. Larvae are shaped similarly to ladybeetle larvae, but are pale cream with brown markings and obvious curved mandibles (jaws) for grabbing larger prey. Unlike most other predators, which are seasonal, lacewings stay around from spring to winter.

Ladybeetles and larvae. The adult ladybeetle has a round reddish body and dark spots. It lays tiny orange eggs in tight clusters. The larvae have a tapered shape, somewhat resembling an alligator, with dark bluish-gray and orange coloring. The pupal stage is round and looks like black and orange bird droppings. The adult is an effective predator of aphids, but larvae are even more voracious.

Minute pirate bugs. So small (one-eighth inch or less) they may go unnoticed, these tiny bugs may be found in flowers attacking thrips. Adults are black with white patches on the wings that create a triangular pattern when the wings are at rest. Soft-bodied nymphs are orange and may be mistaken for aphids.

Parasitic wasps and flies. There are many species of these insects, and they are usually extremely specific about which insects they attack. *Trichogramma* wasps attack butterfly and moth eggs and are released in farms to control cabbage looper and hornworm caterpillars. Another type of parasitic wasp deposits an egg within the body of an aphid. When the egg hatches, the larva consumes the aphid from the inside out. The larva pupates and eventually cuts a hole in the aphid body to emerge as an adult wasp. It leaves behind a brown, dry shell called an "aphid mummy."

Praying mantids. Although they are not the most reliable form of control because they will eat just about anything, praying mantids are fascinating to observe. Adults are pale green or brown, two to three inches long, with large eyes and even a charming head tilt as they examine their surroundings. Strong legs grab prey and hold it in an upright "prayer" position while the unfortunate victim is consumed. Eggs are laid in a mass and protected in a brown foam-like substance that dries hard. The young hatch and emerge from the egg case in a hoard, ready to eat. If nothing else is at hand, they will consume each other.

Predatory wasps. Wasps, such as the mud dauber, capture and eat their prey and also feed it to their offspring in the same way that birds feed their young. Wasps consume caterpillars.

Spiders. Spiders are generally recognizable with their eight legs and shapely hourglass bodies. They sometimes get a bad rap in the media, starring in creepy movies about arachnids running amok. In Arizona, black widow spiders and Arizona brown spiders have venom that can cause severe health problems in humans. Otherwise, spider species are excellent predators to have around because they perform a tremendous amount of insect control in the garden. You may see a cockroach dangling from the web of a black widow. As another bonus, hummingbirds use spiders' sticky web material to make their nests. Leave a few cobwebs hanging in outdoor windows and you can view the birds up close as they hover and collect the silk.

Many spider species build webs to capture prey but some choose other methods. For example, giant crab spiders hunt cockroaches and crickets at night. They construct a hollow ball from their web silk, about the size of a golf ball, to crawl into for protection during the day. Another type of crab spider hides in a flower waiting for unsuspecting prey. It camouflages itself by changing color to match the flower. Crab spiders are easy to identify because they have legs that face forward, resembling crabs at the beach. Other beneficial arachnids are the jumping spiders. There are many species and some are very colorful. They stalk around on hairy legs looking for prey, jump on the unsuspecting victim, and grasp it with their strong legs. They can be identified by the four large eyes on their face and four small eyes on top of their head.

Sun spiders. These spider relatives resemble scorpions and can "run like the wind" to catch insect prey, which accounts for their other common name, "wind scorpions." Tannish and about an inch or two long, they have noticeable front-end pinchers. Despite their appearance, they are not venomous. They are often attracted to lights at night in search of insect prey.

Spined soldier bugs. Shaped somewhat like a shield, these pale brown bugs have a short sharp spine on each side of their body. Another common name is "stink bug." They eat eggs, nymphs, and adult moths.

Syrphid fly larvae. Adults are often called "flower flies" or "hover flies" because they are found hovering over flowers, feeding on nectar and pollen. Their bodies are black or brown with yellow bands that resemble bees, although they do not sting and are considered good pollinators. They do not eat insects, but lay eggs near aphids. When the larvae (maggots) hatch, they have a ready source of food. Syrphid fly larvae consume up to 400 aphids during their lifecycle.

Whipscorpions. These creatures are in the arachnid family along with spiders and scorpions. They can reach three inches in length and have a long, whiplike tail but have no venom and are not dangerous. However, they can shoot acetic acid (vinegar) from a rear gland as protection from enemies, which gained them the common name of "vinegaroons." They are nocturnal predators, eating a variety of insects. There are also tail-less whipscorpions.

Attracting Beneficial Insects to Your Yard

Many beneficial predators, such as ladybeetles and praying mantids, can be purchased from nurseries, specialty mail-order companies, or Internet sites. There is no guarantee that the insects will stay put once released! If they don't have an adequate food supply, or if other environmental conditions are not to their liking, they'll disappear quickly or be unable to reproduce.

Although it can be an entertaining and educational activity with children to release these insects (watching a hoard of tiny praying mantids exit from their egg case is fun even for adults), it is probably more effective to create a habitat that encourages a diverse insect population. The best way to do that is to eliminate pesticide use. In particular, avoid broad-spectrum pesticides that will kill everything.

Another strategy is to plant nectar- or pollen-producing flowers. Parasitic wasps live longer with a ready source of nectar; therefore, they can lay more eggs in pest populations. Plants from the sunflower family (blanket flower, coreopsis, cosmos, sunflower, yarrow) and carrot family (Queen Anne's lace, bishop's flower, cilantro, dill, fennel) are easy-to-grow choices that attract beneficial insects.

Another effective method is to allow some aphids to multiply on a vigorous plant that is unlikely to be damaged, such as oleander. The presence of aphids attracts predators and parasites to the area.

Earth-Friendly Gardener

Desert milkweeds have been a great plant for attracting beneficial insects into the yard of entomologist and Master Gardener Roberta Gibson. Yellow oleander aphids that get on the milkweeds at certain times of the year are "hosts" to parasitic wasps, green lacewings, ladybeetles, and flower fly larvae. "None of our vegetables or other landscape plants ever have aphids because of this reservoir of beneficial insects," she explains. The milkweeds also attract praying mantids, which are a pale green and match the plant exactly. "We have one praying mantis per plant all summer long," says Gibson. "In fact, these milkweeds have so many interesting insects that neighborhood children arrive with jars to visit our plants!"

Biological Controls and Their Prey

Assassin bugs*	aphids, beetles, caterpillars, stinkbugs
Big-eyed bugs & nymphs*	aphids, caterpillars, leafhoppers, mites, thrips, whiteflies, insect eggs
Centipedes	beetles, cockroaches, crickets, cutworms
Damsel bugs & nymphs*	aphids, caterpillars, leafhoppers, mites
Green lacewing larvae*	aphids, beetles, caterpillars, mealy bugs, spider mites, thrips, whiteflies
Ladybeetles & larvae	aphids, mealybugs, mites, scales
Minute pirate bugs	spider mites, thrips
Parasitic wasps	aphids, caterpillars, grasshoppers
Praying mantids*	eats just about everything, including each other
Predatory wasps	bees, caterpillars, spiders
Spiders*	many insects and spiders
Spined soldier bugs	beetles, caterpillars
Sun spiders*	beetles, flies, leafhoppers, moths
Syrphid fly larvae	aphids
Whipscorpions*	beetles, cockroaches, crickets, cutworms

*Will eat just about any insect, mite, or spider of suitable size.

A Bug's Life

All insects undergo changes in shape during their life cycle, a process called "metamorphosis." Some insect species have four distinct body forms that look quite different from each other. This is the "complex metamorphosis" experienced by butterflies, moths, flies, wasps, ants, and beetles. The adult lays an egg that hatches as a caterpillar or grub, which is referred to as the larval stage. The larva eats voraciously, preparing itself to pupate, which is basically a resting stage. The pupa changes shape to emerge as the adult who lays eggs to start the cycle anew. The larva and adult usually eat different things. For example, butterflies sip flower nectar while the caterpillars chew plant foliage.

Other insect species such as aphids, true bugs, and grasshoppers go through a "simple metamorphosis" in which there are just three stages. They hatch from an egg as a nymph and grow to be an adult. The nymph looks a lot like the adult but lacks wings and is smaller in size. The nymph and adult usually feed on the same things. It is important to learn to recognize insects in each of their forms so you can identify friend from foe.

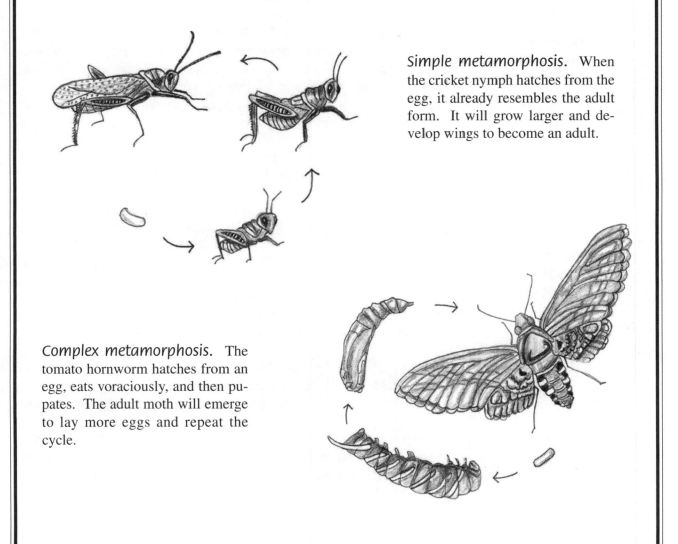

Simple metamorphosis. When the cricket nymph hatches from the egg, it already resembles the adult form. It will grow larger and develop wings to become an adult.

Complex metamorphosis. The tomato hornworm hatches from an egg, eats voraciously, and then pupates. The adult moth will emerge to lay more eggs and repeat the cycle.

Chemical Controls

Chemical control is the method of last resort, after you have tried all strategies to no avail and have decided that the pest is creating more havoc than you or your plants can tolerate. Unfortunately, many pesticides indiscriminately kill all insects, including beneficial pollinators, predators, butterflies, and moths. Pesticides can also be harmful to birds, frogs, lizards, and other small wildlife that consume large quantities of insects free of charge and are an important part of the food chain. Pesticides can disrupt nature's own control methods and the targeted pests tenaciously build up resistance over time, so try all other methods first.

In 1997, Americans used 136,000,000 pounds of active chemical ingredients in various home and garden pesticides, according to the EPA. This included herbicides, insecticides, miticides, fungicides, fumigants, nematicides, and sulfur/oil. Combined with commercial and agricultural use, the number rises to 1.23 billion pounds of active chemical ingredients used in 1997 (most current figures available). We can all contribute to reducing reliance on pesticides by following an IPM program.

Should You Spray Pesticides Regularly?

It is unnecessary to apply pesticides monthly or bi-monthly as part of a routine maintenance program or as preventive treatment. This procedure kills beneficial insects and throws nature's intricate system out of balance. Think of the application of pesticides to the environment as similar to humans taking antibiotics. It isn't advisable to take an antibiotic regularly to prevent a cold or disease. Such a practice is an unnecessary expense. Germs develop resistance when antibiotics are overused. The antibiotics can cause secondary health problems, and you may never even be exposed to a disease.

Similar reasoning applies to regular pesticide use. It is an unnecessary expense. Pests have already developed resistance to many pesticides and will continue to do so. Spraying for one pest kills beneficials that control that or other pests. Finally, pests usually disappear on their own due to changes in climate or the appearance of beneficial insects.

Most synthetic pesticides have temporary results. It is more effective in the long run to encourage a diverse group of insect species to take up residence in your yard by planting a wide variety of plants.

Using Pesticides Responsibly

If you must use a pesticide, do so responsibly. Inappropriately applied pesticides can contaminate our water sources and kill wildlife, birds, and fish. The Arizona Department of Environmental Quality has detected pesticides in groundwater supplies throughout the state. Before purchasing, read the label, even the miniscule print. Ensure that it is formulated for the pest you want to target. All pesticides do not work on all pests. If possible, choose a product that is target-specific, rather than a broad-spectrum chemical that will kill everything. Buy only enough product for a specific use. Follow application and storage instructions exactly. Don't

---

Words on Pesticide Labels

Broad-spectrum: Kills many pests, including beneficials.

Selective: Targets a specific pest or pests. Selective products are a better choice.

pour unused product into drains and toilets or onto the ground. Take it to a hazardous waste disposal site. Call your city or county solid waste department for locations near you.

Organic Versus Synthetic Pesticides

Organic pesticides are made from naturally occuring plants, animals, or minerals. Examples include rotenone and pyrethrum (insecticides derived from plants), *Bacillus thuringiensis* (bacteria that kill specific insects), and Bordeaux (fungicide made from rock minerals). Synthetic chemicals are "synthesized" and contain carbon and hydrogen in their basic structure. Examples include glyphosate (herbicide) and pyrethroids (insecticide).

All pesticides are toxic by definition (they kill) and there are organic pesticides that are more toxic than synthetics. Toxicity is measured by how much of a substance is required to kill half of the targeted pest population. The smaller the amount required, the more toxic the substance is. Nicotine, an insecticide derived from plants, has one of the highest toxicity levels of any pesticide. However, measures of toxicity do not take into account potential health or environmental hazards. As a general rule, the organic pesticides will break down faster than the synthetics and are less likely to remain in the environment to contaminate soil or water supplies.

Watch the Weather

Weather conditions during application can reduce a pesticide's effectiveness and unnecessarily put the substance into the surrounding environment. Read product labels carefully for instructions on use. Watch out for:

- ❑ Wind. Don't spray if wind speeds are over 10 miles per hour. Pesticide drift can damage nearby plants and create cranky neighbors.

- ❑ Temperature. Some chemicals volatilize (turn to gas) when temperatures are high. They must be applied in morning or evening, when it is cool.

- ❑ Rain or sprinklers. Water applied too soon after pesticide application may wash it off before it has time to work. The resulting runoff contaminates the water supply.

- ❑ Ultraviolet light. Many chemicals are deactivated by ultraviolet light, so they must be applied in the evening.

Weed Control

Use a thick layer of mulch to inhibit germination and growth. Pull or hoe weeds as soon as they appear. Quick eradication keeps their population in check. Dig out weeds that spread by underground runners.

Don't let weeds flower and set seed. They produce a multitude of seeds as a survival mechanism, which can remain in the soil indefinately waiting to sprout when conditions are to their liking. Toss the green foliage (not the seedheads) into the compost pile as a good source of nitrogen.

Earth-Friendly Gardener

Master Gardener Michelle Rauscher, co-author of *Desert Landscaping for Beginners*, found that just about any insect problem resolved itself if pesticides were not sprayed. Eliminating their use in the garden allowed her to observe the intricate web of life that constantly seeks to bring itself into balance. If aphids were sucking the juices from tender shoots, beneficial insects such as ladybeetles or green lacewings were soon consuming them. Seasonal changes created inhospitable living conditions that depleted pest populations. When she was occasionally tempted to apply a pesticide years ago, reading the long list of warnings on the label convinced her to put the bottle back on the shelf. "We may not be able to greatly influence large-scale pollution, but we can control what happens on our own plots of land," she says.

It should seldom be necessary to spray an herbicide to control weeds in the home landscape if you keep on top of the situation.

Corn gluten meal, a by-product of the corn milling process, works as a natural pre-emergent herbicide. Iowa State University researcher Nick Christians discovered that the meal stops root formation as seeds germinate. Without a root system, they can't survive. Timing of the application is crucial. After weeds germinate, the corn gluten meal won't stop the plant from growing. Because the meal is about 10 percent nitrogen, it also acts as a fertilizer for weeds or other plants that have already germinated, basically creating a natural "weed and feed" product. Research showed that corn gluten was effective against 22 common weeds including monocots (grasses) and dicots (broad-leaf) such as crabgrass, dandelions, pigweed, purslane, and lambsquarters. It can be used on lawns as well as flower and vegetable gardens. Follow product directions for application rates, also making sure that it works against the weeds you want to target.

Weed Killer

White vinegar sprayed on weeds will kill them. It works best on summer weeds such as spurge, purslane, and pigweed. Be careful not to overspray on desirable plants.

Integrated Pest Management Examples for the Low Desert

Described below are insects that appear in the low desert during the cool season or warm season. Most are harmless although the insect or their "handiwork" may be highly noticeable; some have the potential to become problems. The months in which they usually appear provide a guideline to help identify what is in your garden, although you may see them at other times or not at all because insect activity is dependent on weather conditions and temperatures. Control methods from an IPM perspective are covered from the least to most aggressive. No Control is always an option, as many insect populations will decline with changes in weather. Cultural Control assumes that you are already providing appropriate plant care so in most cases is not repeated here; cultural factors that might influence a specific situation are mentioned.

Insects That May Appear in the Cool Season

Aphids
Signs and Symptoms: Tiny, soft insects found on the growing tips and buds of many annual plants and shrubs. Plants have a sticky honeydew residue, and in severe cases, plants may yellow and wilt.
Months: February–April and October–November.
Insect: Aphids are tiny (one-sixteenth inch), soft-bodied insects that cluster on tender new growth to suck plant sap. There are numerous aphid species, each with preferred plants. Aphid coloration varies, including green, dark grey, and even bright yellow.

No Control: Leave them to attract beneficial biological controls, which are good for the overall health and diversity of your landscape.

Cultural: Don't overwater and overfertilize, which produces a flush of tender, nutrient-rich growth to attract the aphids.

Mechanical: Squish small numbers between your fingers. Spray plants with a blast of water from the hose.

Biological: Ladybeetles, ladybeetle larvae, green lacewing larvae, parasitic wasps, syrphid fly larvae. Aphid "mummies" are aphids that have been parasitized. Parasitic wasps deposit their eggs inside the aphid. When the larva hatches, it feeds inside the living aphid. It eventually releases substances that cause the aphid to harden and turn brown. Leave mummies alone as the parastic wasps will emerge as adults to lay eggs inside more aphids.

Chemical: Use a soapy water spray. (Although detergent is less toxic than a synthetic pesticide, when it is used with water as an insecticide, it is technically classified as a chemical control.)

Cabbage Loopers

Signs and Symptoms: Irregular holes or ragged edges on leaves, most often older leaves of beets, broccoli, Brussels sprouts, cauliflower, celery, collards, kale, lettuce, peas, potatoes, radishes, tomatoes, and turnips. They also bore holes in lettuce and cabbage heads.

Months: October–December.

Insect: Cabbage loopers are pale green caterpillars that are one to two inches long with white stripes on their backs. They are easily identified by the little arch they make with their bodies as they crawl. The adult moths are brown and gray, about one and a half inches. They have silver spots on their upper wings. Dome-shaped eggs with ridges are laid singly on the undersides of older leaves.

No Control: Leave for the birds to eat.

Cultural: Remove weeds that harbor loopers.

Mechanical: Row covers inhibit adult moths from laying eggs. Look beneath leaves for eggs and destroy. Handpick caterpillars.

Biological: *Bacillus thuringiensus* (Bt), damsel bugs, parasitic wasps, spiders.

Chemical: Best not to spray edible plants.

Leafhoppers

Signs and Symptoms: Young vegetable plants are severely stunted and die, while older plants turn yellow, leaves roll upward, fruit production ceases, and plants slowly die. This is curly top virus, which is spread by the leafhopper as it sucks plant sap and moves from plant to plant. The insect's feeding damage is minimal, but the virus will strike more than 150 species, including tomatoes, beans, melons, and beets.

Months: March for tomatoes; summer for grape leafhoppers and citrus.

Insect: Leafhoppers are wedge-shaped, about 1/8 inch long, with strong legs for moving from plant to plant. They are also capable of flight.

No Control: Leave for hummingbirds to eat.

Mechanical: Leafhoppers like warm, sunny places so cover tomatoes and other susceptible crops with floating row covers or provide other shade. Because they are so mobile, leafhoppers may be difficult to control.

Biological: Long-legged flies.

Thrips

Signs and Symptoms: Citrus leaves curl and fruit has external scars. Rose petal edges are brown.

Months: Thrips feed on the new flush of citrus leaves, green stems, and small fruit in February and March. Thrips hide in newly forming rose buds and feed on the petals in April–June and to a lesser extent with the second bloom period in October. Thrips are usually gone before the damage is noticed.

Insect: There are many species of thrips, although citrus thrips and flower thrips in the low desert usually create only cosmetic damage with their rasping mouthparts. Citrus thrips are slender yellowish insects about 1/20 inch long; flower thrips are two times longer and a darker brownish shade. The wings of adults have a fringe of hairs when viewed under a hand lens. Shake citrus blossoms or rose buds over a piece of white paper and look for tiny insects that resemble wood splinters.

No Control: Damage is usually cosmetic and does not reduce citrus fruit's internal quality. Spraying destroys pollinators. Improperly timed insecticide treatments can drastically reduce fruit yield.

Cultural: Healthy plants outlast damage.

Biological: Minute pirate bugs.

Chemical: Should only be needed if roses are to be exhibited in shows. Spray an insecticide such as orthene on the unopened buds, not the entire bush.

Insects That May Appear in the Warm Season

Agave Weevil

Signs and Symptoms: Agave plants collapse into a putrid mess.

Months: Agaves collapse in September, although the adult beetle may be seen walking around the base of agaves in late spring/early summer, usually May.

Insect: The adult beetle is black, about one inch long, with a long curved snout. It feeds on agaves, at the same time introducing a bacteria that seems to be needed for its larvae to develop. The beetle then lays eggs in the feeding holes. The larvae hatch and do more damage by burrowing and eating into the plant's center. Larvae look like white grubs without legs.

No Control: Not a good option as the beetles will spread to nearby agaves. When an infected agave shows signs of decline, it is too late to save it.

Cultural: Remove all diseased agaves, including surrounding soil that may harbor the larvae.

Mechanical: Squash the adult beetles.

Chemical: If you see beetles, treat all agaves in the area with a liquid or granular insecticide targeted for beetles and grubs.

Carpenter Bees

Signs and Symptoms: Large black bees are flying around.

Months: March–April.

Insect: Carpenter bees are about one inch long and as wide as a thumb. The females are a dark bluish-black color. The males are tan or blond. The female is capable of stinging but is unlikely to do so unless threatened. They are solitary bees that make their tunnel-like nests in unfinished wood, such as firewood and dead trees. They do not bother painted or finished wood.

No Control: Leave these bees alone as they are good pollinators.

Mechanical: Remove dead wood from trees. Cover firewood with a tarp. Paint or seal exterior woods on buildings regularly.

Caterpillars (Migrating)

Signs and Symptoms: Hoards of fuzzy caterpillars crawl across the landscape, covering roads, lawns, and even swimming pools.

Months: September.

Insect: Several species, including armyworms, white-lined sphinx, and salt marsh caterpillars, may perform this ritual when their natural habitat of roadside weeds and cotton fields is defoliated. They usually won't do much damage to your plants, as they are searching for a good place to pupate.

No Control: Best method, as they will soon disappear or be eaten by birds.

Cultural: Clean up weeds.

Mechanical: Handpick, scoop out of pools, use a foil or metal barrier for specific areas.

Biological: Many beneficial insects or diseases attack caterpillars.

Cicadas

Signs and Symptoms: A loud buzzing and humming sound fills the air. Dried, brown insect "bodies" stick to trees and walls or are found on the ground beneath trees. Mesquite and other trees have scarring on young twigs that resembles tiny knife cuts every 4–10 inches along the branch. Branches may die back from the tip.

Months: May–August.

Insect: Adult cicadas are two inches long with chunky bodies and protruding eyes. Wings fold over their backs. The female cicada creates the scars in tender wood by making a small slit in which to deposit her eggs. The damage may cause the branch tip to die and even fall off. When the eggs hatch, the nymphs drop to the ground and burrow into the soil in search of food, eventually emerging again in two to three years as soft-bodied adults encased in an outer shell, called an exoskeleton. They shed the exoskeleton, harden their bodies, and are ready for flight. Male cicadas create the noisy din by vibrating their rib plates to attract females for mating.

No Control: No management is needed. It should be considered natural pruning that does not harm, and may actually be beneficial to, the tree. Also, the adult does not feed so would not ingest any type of insecticide.

Biological: Adults are a veritable feast for birds. You can also collect the soft, non-moving nymphs to feed to your insect-eating pets.

Cochineal Scale

Signs and Symptoms: White, fluffy looking substance spreads across prickly pear and cholla cacti.

Months: Year around.
Insect: A barely visible scale insect secretes the white substance as protection. The insect is a scarlet color and people traditionally collected it to make a natural dye. In Mexico, the scale is today grown on prickly pear pads in nurseries and "harvested."

No Control: Harvest the scale for dye.
Mechanical: Wash off with a strong spray of water from the hose. Repeat as needed.
Biological: Ladybeetles, syrphid flies, green lacewing larvae.

Cutworms

Signs and Symptoms: Seedlings are cut off at the base.
Months: November–February.
Insect: A brownish-grayish caterpillar that lives just below the soil surface and comes out at night to feed. Because they are seldom seen, other creatures such as birds and pillbugs get blamed for their damage.

Mechanical: Protect seedlings with cardboard collars around their base. Gently dig in the soil with your finger where damage is seen because cutworms are usually close by. Look under clods of soil and plant debris. Handpick and dispose of them.

Darkling Beetles

Signs and Symptoms: Large numbers of small dark beetles cluster around lights or moist areas and may get into the house.
Months: May to September, especially July.
Insect: Darkling beetles are one-quarter to one-half inch long and have hard, dull brown or bluish-black shells. They live in the soil and recycle dead organic matter. When the soil dries out in summer and weeds dry up, they may move in mass migrations for more favorable habitat. They often seek shelter indoors.

No Control: They are seasonal and will disappear on their own.
Cultural: Larvae feed on weeds, so remove weeds.
Mechanical: If indoors, vacuum them up.

False Chinch Bugs

Signs and Symptoms: Large clusters of dull-colored bugs suddenly appear.
Months: April.
Insect: False chinch bugs have narrow, grayish-brown bodies that are less than one-quarter inch long. They cluster together in high numbers to prepare for migration to higher elevations. They do no harm to people or landscape plants, but their sheer numbers may be a nuisance.

No Control: They usually disappear as rapidly as they arrived.
Cultural: Timing of weed control can help prevent large populations of false chinch bugs from appearing in April. They feed on London Rocket and other weeds in the mustard family in January and February. Pull these weeds as soon as they appear and eliminate their food source. Rainy winters encourage weed growth, which promotes the false chinch bug population.

Fig Beetles and Green June Beetles

Signs and Symptoms: Chubby green beetles are flying around, often near fruit trees. White grubs are found in the soil. (See also June Beetles.)
Months: July–August.
Insect: Fig beetles and green June beetles are members of the *Cotinus* genus and have similar habits and appearance. They are one inch long with bright green bodies. They eat figs, apricots, peaches, and prickly pear fruit and can decimate fruit quickly. The larval stage is a fat two-inch white grub that flops onto its back and crawls along using hairs on its back. Larvae are often found in the midst of compost piles, where they are considered beneficial because they are breaking down organic matter.

Mechanical: Put paper bags around fruit before it starts to ripen.

Flea Beetles

Signs and Symptoms: Tiny pin-prick holes appear on the foliage of a variety of vegetables. Mexican evening primrose foliage looks tattered.
Months: Spring, when Mexican primrose is thriving. Some species may attack cool-season vegetables at other elevations.
Insect: Flea beetle adults are tiny beetles ranging from 1/16 to 1/4 inch long. Different species are black, greenish- or bluish-black, green, or yellow and may be shiny. There common name derives from their ability to jump like fleas with their enlarged hind legs when disturbed. Larvae are grayish-green worms that have dark heads and resemble caterpillars.

Cultural: Maintain healthy plants. Because the holes they create by feeding are so tiny, damage can be outgrown if plants are otherwise strong. One species of flea beetle attacks Mexican evening primrose vigorously. This plant is a hardy spreading plant. If in full sun to promote growth, it usually outcompetes the beetle.

Mechanical: Wash off with a spray of water.

Grape Leaf Skeletonizers

Signs and Symptoms: Grape leaves are decimated, with just a "skeleton" of plant tissue left behind.

Months: March–May.

Insect: Adult moth is shiny, bluish-black, and about one inch long. It lays masses of yellow eggs on undersides of grape leaves in late spring. They hatch into pretty, although voracious, bluish-black and yellow caterpillars who devour foliage in groups, leaving only the veins of foliage in their wake.

No Control: The larval stage (caterpillar) can quickly decimate foliage if not controlled.

Cultural: Don't plant grapes.

Mechanical: Monitor grapevines regularly in late spring and destroy adult moths and eggs. Handpick caterpillars. Use gloves and a dust mask for protection because caterpillars have stinging "hairs" that can break off and cause a skin reaction or be inhaled.

Biological: *Bacillus thuringiensus* (Bt), parasitic wasps.

Chemical: Carbaryl.

June Beetles/White Grubs

Signs and Symptoms: Brownish beetles about one-half inch long are flying around lights at night. White grubs are found in garden soil, compost piles, and turf. (See also Fig Beetles.)

Months: Adults, April–June. Grubs, year around.

Insect: The adult beetle is a "scarab" beetle similar in shape to the fig beetle or green June beetle, although slightly smaller. The larval stage is a white grub with a tan head that curls into a "C" shape. There are many species of scarab beetles whose larval stage is a white grub. Some grubs prefer a specific location, such as the fig beetle, which chooses a compost pile to break down organic matter. Others are pests, consuming the roots of turf, ornamental plants, and vegetables.

Cultural: Adults are mainly nocturnal. Turn off outside lights.

Mechanical: Handpick the grubs when cultivating the soil.

Leafcutter Bees

Signs and Symptoms: Semi-circular or half-moon cut-outs appear on the edges of smooth leaves or petals such as bougainvillea and roses.

Months: April–June.

Insect: Leafcutter bees are slightly smaller than honeybees. The female transports the neatly cut foliage to a small hole that is just slightly larger than her body. There she constructs a nest; fills it with pollen and nectar mixed into a ball to feed her young; lays one egg per nest; and seals it up with more cut-outs.

No Control: Damage is aesthetic. These are solitary bees, each building nests and rearing their young, so swarming bees are not a factor. Bees are excellent pollinators.

Mechanical: Erect floating row covers over plants if appearance is important, such as roses that will be exhibited in shows.

Biological: Natural predators and parasites.

Chemical: Since they do not ingest the plant tissue, chemical controls are not effective.

Orange Dog Caterpillars

Signs and Symptoms: Something that resembles bird droppings is on citrus foliage.

Months: May–September (often coincides with a new flush of foliage growth).

Insect: This is a caterpillar that displays mottled brownish-gray and white colors as a natural camouflage to hide from predators. The adult is the beautiful black and yellow giant swallowtail butterfly.

No Control: Larvae seldom eat enough foliage to damage a healthy tree. Leave them alone to become butterflies.

Mechanical: Handpick.

Biological: Variety of natural parasites attack the eggs and small caterpillars. Only a few reach maturity.

Palm Flower Caterpillars

Signs and Symptoms: Caterpillars are crawling around underneath palm trees, usually fan palms, or may even be found indoors.

Months: June–September, when palms have flowers.
Insect: Palm flower caterpillars are one inch long and come in a variety of pink/brown/cream shades. The adult moth is tan and has two dark circles on the edges of its rear wings. It lays eggs on palm flower stalks. The caterpillars don't do damage feeding on palm flowers. They build cocoons and pupate under the palm peels. Sometimes caterpillars are dislodged by winds or by pruning the flower stalks, so they seek another place to pupate. If they crawl indoors, they chew carpets, upholstery, and books to obtain fiber to build their cocoon.

Cultural: Timing the pruning of flower stalks, called spathes, can prevent problems. Prune in early spring (April–May) before the flowers begin opening and adult moths lay their eggs on them. Alternatively, wait until the spathe has finished flowering usually towards the end of July. If pruning in spring, leave at least five rows of peels to provide shelter for the caterpillars.
Mechanical: Handpick caterpillars. Seal and caulk cracks around windows and doors.

Palo Verde Root Borers

Signs and Symptoms: Large (three to four inches) black beetles with long antennae are flying around. Smooth-sided holes the size of a quarter are in the ground beneath the canopies of native palo verde trees as well as many non-native trees. Branches may die back.
Months: June–August.
Insect: The adult palo verde beetle lays eggs in the ground beneath trees. When they hatch, the larvae eat the tree roots and grow into whitish grubs five inches long and one inch wide. They live below ground for three years, finally emerging as adult beetles.

Cultural: Maintain healthy trees with appropriate watering and fertilizer if needed, as the beetles attack stressed trees. No other controls.

Palo Verde Webworms

Signs and Symptoms: Web-like structures, usually in palo verde or Texas mountain laurel trees, provide safe haven during the day for a thin, half-inch long caterpillar. The caterpillars feed on tender foliage at night.
Months: April, when the palo verde trees begin leafing out.

Insect: Palo verde "webbers" tend to congregate in groups, so the whitish webbing all over a tree looks worse than it is. They do little permanent damage as these trees are well-adapted.

Mechanical: Cut off the smaller stems that hold the webs.
Biological: Caterpillars make good bird food. Spray at night with *Bacillus thuringiensis* (Bt).

Psyllids

Signs and Symptoms: A sticky residue is all over desert trees, including palo verde and ironwood.
Months: April–May, in some years.
Insect: Psyllids are one-quarter inch long, somewhat round on each end. Their coloring blends in with foliage. They are cyclical, appearing in large numbers some years but not others. When populations are high, their sap-sucking leaves honeydew residue on the tree.

Mechanical: Spray off the foliage with water.
Chemical: Spraying an insecticide upwards into the canopy of a tree is not a safe method, as the chemical will drift. Psyllids, like aphids and whiteflies, may succumb to a spray of soapy water.

Spider Mites

Signs and Symptoms: Fine threads that look like spider webbing cover the foliage. Leaves have yellow spots and may be deformed with twisting and stunting.
Months: May–October.
Insects: Mites are tiny round or oval arachnids with eight legs, usually too small to be seen without a microscope. They may be yellow, red, greenish, or brownish in color.

Cultural: They thrive in dusty conditions so wash off foliage with a spray of water from the hose.
Mechanical: Hose off mites with water.
Chemical: Use a soapy water spray. Miticides.

Spittle Bugs

Signs and Symptoms: Small white "spit balls" show up on rosemary, sage, other woody perennials, and bean-producing desert trees including palo verde, ironwood, and mesquite.
Months: May–September.
Insect: A small insect called a spittle bug produces

this foam to protect itself from predators while it sucks plant sap with piercing mouth parts. Spittle bugs cause very little damage to healthy plants.

Cultural: Maintain healthy plants.
Mechanical: Hose off with water.

Tomato (Tobacco) Hornworm

Signs and Symptoms: The leaves on tomatoes, peppers, eggplant, tobacco, and other leafy plants have ragged holes.
Months: June–August.
Insect: These bright green caterpillars display white stripes and a decorative "horn" that projects from the rear. Tobacco and tomato hornworms appear very similar, and the names are often used interchangeably, although they are different species. Hornworms are about three inches long and one-half inch wide. Their green coloration blends so well with foliage that they can be difficult to detect; however, dark pellets of fecal matter give away their location. The caterpillar burrows into the soil to pupate. The pupa is dark reddish-brown and cigar shaped. The adult moth is two inches long, grayish-brown with pale markings. At first glance it might be mistaken for a hummingbird, as it hovers over flowers at dusk using a long tongue to reach the nectar.

No Control: Leave for the birds to eat.
Mechanical: Handpick caterpillars. Look for pupae in soil when cultivating and destroy them.
Biological: *Bacillus thuringiensus* (Bt), damsel bugs, parasitic wasps, spiders.
Chemical: Best not to spray edible plants.

Whiteflies

Signs and Symptoms: Plants sticky with honeydew; leaves yellowing and wilting.
Months: August–October for the silverleaf whitefly, which is most common. Other types appear at other times of year.
Insect: Adult whiteflies are tiny (less than one-sixteenth inch) flying insects with sucking mouth parts. They are usually on the underside of foliage and fly off if the plant is disturbed, although they soon return. The immature stage is round, flat, and immobile, resembling a drop of water or a scale insect. It is also sucking sap from the plant. The immatures may be less susceptible to conventional insecticides because of the

way they are protected on the underside of the leaves.

No Control: Cool weather will knock their population down to reasonable numbers.
Cultural: Wait to plant cool-season vegetable crops until October when whitefly populations decrease with colder weather.
Mechanical: Wash off foliage, especially the undersides, with a strong spray of water from the hose. Repeat as needed. Erect yellow sticky traps, although some experts suggest that sticky traps do not greatly decrease the whitefly population, but rather serve as an effective monitoring device to determine if the numbers are declining.
Biological: Big-eyed bugs, green lacewings, parasitic wasps.
Chemical: Use a soapy water spray. Repeat every three to four days. ✳

Appendices

Checklists

Water Conservation
Green Waste Reduction
Energy Efficiency
Water Quality Preservation
Wildfire-Defensive Landscape
Edible Landscape and Worksheet
Edible Plant Varieties
Wildlife Habitat Checklist and Worksheet
Plant Selection Checklist and Worksheet
Site Assessment/Base Map

Landscape Watering Guidelines

Earth-Friendly Guide for Watering and Fertilizing Lawns

Plant Lists

Resources

These checklists provide the basic steps for topics covered in this book. Use them to determine what earth-friendly elements already occur in your landscape and what you'd like to implement next. More information on each subject is included in the book.

Water Conservation Checklist

✓ Planning

❑ Limit turf and pool size.

❑ Go Native! Native plants need less water.

❑ Group plants with similar water needs.

❑ Install an effective irrigation system.

❑ Use organic mulches on the soil surface to reduce evaporation.

❑ Use semi-permeable materials for patios and sidewalks to allow water to soak into the ground rather than run into storm drains.

❑ Add the following methods to capture rainwater:

-Berms
-Swales
-Boomerangs
-Mulch pits
-Rain barrels or other containers

❑ Redirect graywater from tubs, showers, bathroom sinks, and laundry to irrigate landscape.

✓ Maintenance

❑ Replenish organic mulch (bark, wood chips, compost) around plants.

❑ Incorporate organic matter into the soil, which improves its water-holding capacity.

❑ Adjust irrigation timer monthly to correspond to the weather and plants' water needs.

❑ Water lawns from 3 to 6 a.m. to reduce loss from evaporation and wind.

❑ Schedule 10-minute weekly irrigation inspections on your calendar to spot leaks, clogged emitters, and overruns.

❑ Don't overwater. Follow the 1-2-3 Rule. ✳

Green Waste Reduction Checklist

✓ Planning

❑ Choose the "Right Plant for the Right Place." Allowing space for the plant's mature size reduces the need for pruning, which creates green waste.

❑ Plan to use organic mulches instead of hardscape surfaces.

✓ Maintenance

❑ Do not overwater and overfertilize, which stimulate excessive growth.

❑ Minimize pruning. Prune for a specific reason, e.g., to remove a dead branch.

❑ Spread leaves, bark chips, and other green waste as organic mulch.

❑ Leave grass clippings on the lawn to decompose after mowing.

❑ Make compost with landscape trimmings and return organic matter to the soil. ✳

Energy Efficiency Checklist

✓ Planning

❑ Use your site assessment to review the solar exposure and prevailing wind for your landscape.

❑ Determine where solar arcs or windbreaks can be placed to moderate sun and wind.

❑ Provide cover for the south-facing side of your house with deciduous vines on a trellis or ramada to provide shade in summer and allow sunshine to warm the house in winter.

❑ Place evergreen shade trees on the east and west side of the house.

❑ Use plants to shade the air conditioning unit.

❑ Plant shrubs around the foundation of the house (three feet from wall to prevent water damage) to provide shade and "dead air space."

❑ Use evergreen vines on west- and north-facing walls. In addition to shade, their foliage provides an "evaporative cooling" effect. ✳

Water Quality Preservation Checklist

✓ Planning

❑ Choose native and desert plants for the majority of your landscape. They are adapted to existing soil conditions and native insects, thus greatly reducing the amounts of fertilizer and pesticide that may be needed over a plant's lifetime.

❑ Create swales and other water-harvesting earthworks to slow the flow of water, allowing it to soak in around plants. This helps reduce soil erosion, which carries contaminants with it.

❑ Do not use graywater from toilets, kitchen sinks, or dishwashers to water the landscape, as it contains contaminants.

✓ Maintenance

❑ Leave grass clippings on the lawn to decompose. They return up to 25 percent nitrogen to the soil, reducing the amount of fertilizer needed.

❑ Water efficiently. Overwatering may leach nitrogen fertilizer and pesticides into the groundwater.

❑ Check sprinklers and irrigation systems regularly to ensure water is not running off your landscape into the street, eventually carrying fertilizer and pesticide into water sources.

❑ Apply mulch, which helps prevent soil erosion.

❑ Determine the most likely cause of a plant problem before indiscriminately applying fertilizer or pesticide as the "solution."

❑ Use Integrated Pest Management methods to solve insect problems. Use synthetic chemical pesticides only as a last resort.

❑ Follow fertilizer and pesticide product label instructions exactly. Never apply more than the recommended amount.

❑ Dispose of unused pesticides and other chemicals at hazardous waste disposal sites. Don't pour them on the ground or down sinks and toilets. Check with your city's sanitation department for scheduled drop off dates. Buy only as much product as currently needed to eliminate the need for disposal.

❑ Dispose of pet feces properly. ✳

Wildfire-Defensive Landscape Checklist

✓ Maintenance

❑ Elements in the landscape will change over the seasons and over the years, so review your yard's components at least annually to make sure it still meets fire safety objectives.

❑ Maintain your defensible space regularly with good plant care techniques, including proper watering and pruning.

❑ Remove or mow annuals, perennials, and wildflowers after they have gone to seed.

❑ Mow grasses regularly. Keep the height low near any structures. In outlying areas, grasses should grow no taller than six inches. Mow grass low around shrubs or trees to prevent it from becoming a fuel ladder.

❑ Pine needles and dried leaves should not be allowed to accumulate in thick layers in your defensible space, as they easily catch fire. Rake them up and put them in the compost pile.

❑ Prune dead branches and sucker growth from trees. If you live in a forested region, prune limbs up to a height of 10 feet on mature trees in your defensible space. For young trees, allow some low branches to remain evenly spaced around the lower trunk, as they help the tree develop girth and strength. As a general guideline, prune no more than one-third of the tree in any year. Removing more than one-third stresses the tree and reduces its overall health and vigor.

❑ If drought conditions cause water rationing, save plants nearest the house. Determine which plants will need additional irrigation to survive.

❑ As plants grow and spread, thin out dense plant groupings to prevent an uninterrupted fuel supply.

❑ Clean out rain gutters and roof tops of fallen leaves and needles. ✳

Edible Landscape Checklist

✓ Planning

❑ Decide what fruits, vegetables, herbs, flowers, or other edibles you would like to grow and eat.

❑ List edible plants that already exist in your landscape, such as citrus trees. What time of year is the fruit ready to eat?

❑ Use a simple calendar, such as the sample below, to determine other edible plants that will provide fresh produce for a year-around harvest. ✱

Edible Landscape Harvest Worksheet (Example)												
	Jan	Feb	Mar	Apr	May	Jun	Jul	Aug	Sep	Oct	Nov	Dec
Navel orange 'Cara Cara'	X											X
Valencia orange 'Campbell'	X	X	X	X	X							
Apricot 'Katy'					X	X						
Strawberry 'Chandler'				X	X	X	X					
Fig 'Black Mission'								X	X	X		
Mexican tarragon	X									X	X	X
Salad greens	X	X	X	X							X	X

Edible Plant Varieties Recommended for Low Desert Landscapes

This is a partial list of edible plants that grow in the low desert. It focuses on plants that are relatively easy to grow under average conditions and are free of pest or disease problems if properly maintained. Some of the fruits listed include varieties that perform well here. Growers continue to develop and evaluate new varieties that are heat and disease resistant, cold tolerant, have sweeter fruit and fewer seeds. Thus, some varieties may be difficult to find as newer introductions take their place.

Citrus Trees
Sweet Orange: Diller, Hamlin, Marrs, Pineapple, Trovita
Navel Orange: Cara Cara, Fukumoto, Lane Late, Parent Washington
Valencia Orange: Campbell, Delta, Midknight, Olinda
Pigmented (Blood) Orange: Moro, Ruby, Salustiana, Sanguinelli, Tarroco
Mandarin (also called Tangerine): Algerian, Daisy, Dancy, Fairchild, Kinnow
Tangelo: Minneola, Orlando
Grapefruit: Duncan, Flame, Marsh, Redblush, Texas Star Ruby
Grapefruit x Pummelo: Melogold, Oro Blanco
Lemon: Eureka, Lisbon, Ponderosa
Lime: Mexican lime, Tahiti
Kumquat: Fukushu, Meiwa, Nagami
Limequat: Tavares

Deciduous Fruit Trees
Apple: Anna, Golden Dorsett
Apricot: Blenum, Katy, Poppy
Peach: Babcock, Bonanza Miniature, Earligrande, Flordaprince, Tropic Snow
Plum: Gulf Gold, Gulf Ruby, Santa Rosa

Other Fruits
Blackberry: Brazos, Brison, Rosborough, Womack,
Fig: Black Mission, Conadria, White Kadota
Grape: Cardinal, Exotic, Fantasy, Flame seedless, Perlette, Ruby seedless, Thompson seedless
Pomegranate: Wonderful
Strawberry: Camarosa, Chandler, Sequoia, Tioga

Herb Shrubs
Lemon grass (*Cymbopogon citratus*)
Mt. Lemon marigold (*Tagetes lemonii*)
Mexican tarragon (*Tagetes lucida*)
Rosemary
Chaparral sage (*Salvia clevelandii*)

Scented geranium
Lavender
Oregano
Mexican bush oregano (*Lippia graveolens*)
Mexican bush sage (*Salvia leucantha*)

Edible Flowers
Calendula
Chrysanthemum
Daylily
Dianthus
Johnny-jump-up
Nasturium
Pansy
Signet marigold
Viola

Many plants grown primarily for vegetables, herbs, or fruits also have edible flowers, such as Bok Choy, Borage, Broccoli, Chives, Cilantro, Citrus Blossoms, Dill, Garlic, Garlic Chives, Marjoram, Mint, Okra, Onion, Oregano, Pineapple Sage, Rosemary, Sage, Society Garlic, and Squash.

Plants Traditionally Used by Native Americans
Amaranth
Chiltepine
Devil's claw
Fava bean
Mesquite
Prickly pear

Other Edible Plants
Globe artichoke
Jerusalem artichoke (tuberous root)
Peanuts
Pineapple guava
Sweet potato
Sunflower *

Wildlife Habitat Checklist

✓ Planning

❑   Learn what wildlife species live in or migrate through your area and what native plants they use.

❑   Decide what wildlife you would most like to attract.

❑   Determine what your landscape already offers and add to it. It is okay to start small and increase plant variety as time and money permit.

❑   Use a wide variety of plants with staggered bloom times and multiple uses (flowers, seeds, shelter).

❑   Support wildlife in your backyard by providing these four basic elements: food, water, shelter, and nesting sites.

✓ Food

❑   Go Native! Native plants support 10–50 times more species than do non-native plants.

❑   Add plants with red flowers. Hummingbirds can see the color red from a mile away.

❑   Limit pruning. Allow plants to flower and go to seed.

❑   Avoid the use of pesticides. Insects are an important food source. Hummingbirds eat half their weight in nectar and insects daily, including such pests as aphids and whiteflies.

❑   If you use bird feeders, clean them often as they can contribute to the spread of disease.

✓ Water

❑   Keep water clean to prevent the spread of disease. Scrub still water sources, such as birdbaths, every few days with 9 parts water and 1 part bleach. Allow them to dry in the sun.

❑   Provide flat, shallow water sources for butterflies, such as a stone with a slight depression.

❑   Prevent mosquitoes from breeding in water sources by one of the following methods:

-Add fish that feed on mosquito larvae.

-Use "mosquito dunks," which are made of *Bacillus thuringiensis* var. *israelensis*, a biological control method.

❑   Provide a way for small creatures to climb out of deeper water sources, such as stepping stones or a slanted board.

✓ Shelter and Nesting Sites

❑   Plant evergreen trees or shrubs for year-round protection from weather and predators and as nesting sites.

❑   Leave some branches growing low to the ground rather than pruning up the stem or trunk.

❑   Create rock, log, and mulch piles.

❑   Leave dead trees as nesting spots (assuming they are not a fire hazard).

❑   Place flat stones in the sun in a sheltered location for butterflies to rest and warm themselves. They prefer sunny, windless conditions.

❑   Provide a few flat, safe areas with sand or mulch as some bird species like to take "dust baths." ✱

Wildlife Habitat Worksheet (Example) Note how adding one plant and eliminating one maintenance practice can enhance the habitat for a variety of creatures.					
Wildlife to Attract	Existing Food Plants (Season They Provide Food)	Existing Shelter or Nesting Spots	Plants to Add (Season They Provide Food)	Features to Add	Maintenance
Hummingbirds	Desert willow (summer) Penstemon (spring)	Palo verde	Baja red fairy duster (spring-fall) Firebush (summer-winter)	Plan water feature to install next fall.	Eliminate pesticide use. Birds eat insects.
Cactus wrens	Prickly pear cacti (summer fruit)	Prickly pear Palo verde	Baja red fairy duster used to line nests		Same as above
Verdins		Prickly pear Palo verde	Baja red fairy duster used for food and to line nests		Same as above
Ceraunus blue butterflies			Baja red fairy duster flowers are larval food	Shallow saucer with water. Put flat stones in it.	Mark calender to scrub water source every few days. Good task for kids.
Gulf fritillary butterflies			Passion vine foliage as larval food	same as above	same as above
Lizards		Small rock pile left from digging garden	Cat's claw vine on western block wall to provide shelter	Move rocks to low-traffic corner. Put flat rocks on top as sunning spot for butterflies.	Eliminate pesticide use. Lizards eat insects.

Plant Selection Checklist

❑ Use your site assessment information and bubble diagram to determine your yard's conditions and what you want to achieve.

❑ Measure the space in your landscape where you want to install a tree, shrub, or other plant. Allow extra leeway near sidewalks, driveways, pools, and patios, which is especially important with thorny or spiky plants. Don't forget to look skyward for possible obstructions, such as power lines or roof overhangs.

❑ Use the Plant List to help you choose plants that provide benefits that are important to your plan, such as edible fruit, hummingbird attraction, and energy efficiency.

❑ Check reference books and nursery tags to determine what growing conditions a plant requires, especially sun exposure, as well as its average mature height and width. Ask nursery personnel what growing characteristics are typical in your region. Examine plants at botanical gardens and parks. On your daily commute, observe landscaping on state and federal highways which usually feature desert plants. Match your yard's conditions and available space, as well as your needs, with plants that fulfill as many of your requirements as possible.

❑ Consider what changes may take place as plants mature. For example, a tree that provides partial shade for nearby plants the first year or two of growth may create full shade conditions in a few years, which the other plants can't tolerate. It is okay to wait and watch, adding plants over a period of time as you see how the landscape evolves. You might fill in gaps with colorful annuals and containers while other plants grow.

❑ Consider what changes may take place through the seasons, such as flowering, fruiting, foliage color, leaf drop, and seed pods. Plan for year-around interest. ✳

Plant Selection Worksheet (Example)					
Plant Needed	Possible Choices	Sun Exposure	Space Available/ Plant's Mature Size	Water Use	Other Characteristics Wanted
Tree		full	30 x 30	low	Deciduous Attracts hummingbirds Provides summer color
My choice 1.	Desert willow	full	25 x 25	low	Deciduous Hummingbirds feed on nectar Blooms Apr-Sept
2.	Foothill palo verde	full	25 x 25	low	Deciduous Hummingbirds nest in Blooms Apr-May
3.	Sweet acacia	full	25 x 25	low-med	Evergreen Blooms Dec-Feb Fragrant

Site Assessment/Base Map Checklist

❏ Determine Landcare History

❏ Indicate North

❏ Indicate existing buildings

Sun

❏ Angles and positions in summer and winter

❏ Seasonal shadows from buildings

Wind

❏ Prevailing wind direction

❏ Wind tunnels

❏ Frost pockets

Traffic patterns

❏ Wildlife

❏ People

❏ Pets

Slope and Rainwater

❏ How water currently flows and/or collects on your property

❏ Pitch of the roof and flow of water from the roof

❏ High point and the low point of your property

❏ Water flows on or near your property from an outside source

❏ Areas where water tends to accumulate

❏ Direction and approximate degree of slope

❏ Opportunities for harvesting rainwater

Fire & Lightening

❏ Downslope to upslope areas

❏ Opportunities for creating "breaks" in landscape

❏ Existing high-fuel materials

❏ Power lines ✻

		Mar-May	May-Oct	Oct-Dec	Dec-Mar	How Deep
Landscape Watering Guidelines (Days Between Waterings)						
Trees	Desert-adapted	14-30	7-21	14-30	30-60	3 feet
	High-water-use	7-12	7-10	7-12	14-30	3 feet
Shrubs	Desert-adapted	14-30	7-21	14-30	30-45	2 feet
	High-water-use	7-10	5-7	7-10	10-14	2 feet
Groundcovers, Perennials & Vines	Desert-adapted	14-30	7-21	14-30	21-45	1 foot
	High-water-use	7-10	2-5	7-10	10-14	1 foot
Cacti & Succulents		21-45	14-30	21-45	if needed	1 foot
Annuals		3-7	2-5	3-7	5-10	1 foot

Guidelines are for established plants (3 years for trees, 1 year for shrubs and other plants). New plantings require more frequent water.
Adapted from *Landscape Watering by the Numbers*, Donna DiFrancesco and Robyn Baker, Arizona Municipal Water Users Association.

Earth-Friendly Guide for Watering and Fertilizing Lawns

	Non-Overseeded Bermudagrass (Dormant in Cool Months)		Bermudagrass Overseeded with Ryegrass (OSR) in Cool Months	
	Water	Fertilize	Water	Fertilize
January	Monthly 8-10 inches deep	No	Every 5-10 days 4-6 inches deep	Monthly
February	Monthly 8-10 inches deep	No	Every 5-10 days 4-6 inches deep	Monthly
March	Monthly 8-10 inches deep	No	Every 3-5 days 4-6 inches deep	Monthly
April	Every 5-7 days 8-10 inches deep	Monthly	Every 3-5 days 4-6 inches deep	Monthly
May	Every 3-5 days 8-10 inches deep	Monthly	Every 3-5 days 4-6 inches deep	Monthly
June	90 F and up: every 2-3 days 8-10 inches deep	Monthly	90 F and up: every 2-3 days 8-10 inches deep	Monthly
July	90 F and up: every 2-3 days 8-10 inches deep	Monthly	90 F and up: every 2-3 days 8-10 inches deep	Monthly
August	90 F and up: every 2-3 days 8-10 inches deep	Monthly	90 F and up: every 2-3 days 8-10 inches deep	Monthly
September	90 F and up: every 2-3 days Below 90 F: every 3-5 days 8-10 inches deep	Monthly	90 F and up: every 2-3 days Below 90 F: every 3-5 days 8-10 inches deep	No fertilizer 4-6 weeks before overseeding
October	Every 3-7 days 8-10 inches deep	Monthly	New OSR: 3-4 times daily, 5-10 minutes each	No fertilizer before first mowing of rye
November	If dormant, monthly 8-10 inches deep	No	Established OSR: every 3-7 days, 4-6 inches deep	No fertilizer before first mowing of rye
December	Monthly 8-10 inches deep	No	Established OSR: every 4-10 days, 4-6 inches deep	Monthly

Adapted from *Desert Landscaping for Beginners*, Chapter 13, "Growing a Healthy Lawn" by Sharon Dewey.

Plant Lists Key

The plant lists on the following pages include examples to help you discover the beauty and versatility of desert plants. There are many other plants well-suited to desert gardening that we could not include due to lack of space. Use the Resources list to find other books written by local experts that describe hundreds of desert plants. The plants in these lists fulfill the earth-friendly mission and are:

✓ Native or desert-adapted (a few exceptions, particularly edible plants).

✓ Low-water use once established.

✓ Multipurpose, providing benefits such as shade, food, wildlife habitat, and color.

✓ Relatively easy for the homeowner to find at local nurseries or botanical garden sales.

✓ Relatively no-fuss, growing without fertilizer or pest problems.

Energy Efficiency

These plants provide shade or withstand wind.

D = deciduous, dropping their leaves.

E = evergreen.

S = semi-deciduous, dropping some or all of their leaves in certain conditions, such as severe cold.

Water Use

Most plants are drought tolerant or low-water-users once established, although they may require extra watering during summer. Some may live on low water, but look more attractive or bloom more consistently with moderate water. Exceptions which require regular watering are usually non-native food plants, such as fruit trees.

Wildlife Habitat

Although you may choose plants to attract a particular species, such as hummingbirds, native plants almost always provide resources for a wide range of creatures.

Birds

H = hummingbirds.

X = other birds.

Butterflies

L = larval plant for caterpillars.

N = nectar plant for adults.

Edible

Some part of the plant is edible for humans.

Fragrant

Flowers, foliage or both may be fragrant. Most foliage plants require that the leaves be crushed or brushed against to release the scent, so plant where the aroma can be enjoyed, such as near walkways or patios.

Seasonal Color

Plants listed provide periods of significant color from blooms, foliage, or berries. Flowering times may overlap seasons or vary by elevation, weather, and microclimate. If no color is included, that plant's flowers are insignificant.

Thorns

Plants with thorns or spiky edges should be kept away from patios and sidewalks, although that same feature makes them useful for security plantings. Thorny plants are often attractive to birds for shelter and nesting sites to protect them from predators. Consider the planting location carefully before installing thorny plants.

Miscellaneous

Interesting features, such as textured bark or velvety foliage. Plants that need regular fertilizer are also included.

TREES (Botanical Name / Common Name)	Shade	Wind-break	Low	Med	High	Birds	Butter-flies	Edible	Fragrant	Spring Color	Summer Color	Fall Color	Winter Color	Thorns	Miscellaneous
Acacia constricta Whitethorn acacia	D		X			X			flowers	yellow				X	
Acacia farnesiana (smallii) Sweet acacia	E	X	X	X		X			flowers	yellow			yellow	X	lots of seed pods
Acacia stenophylla Shoestring acacia	E	X	X	X											fits narrow places
Acacia willardiana Palo blanco	D		X												papery white bark
Caesalpinia cacalaco Cascalote	S		X			X						yellow	yellow	X	large flower clusters
Celtis reticulata Netleaf hackberry	D	X	X			X	L								nubby bark, twisting form
Cercidium floridum Blue palo verde	D	X	X			H, X				yellow				X	green bark
Cercidium hybrid 'Desert Museum'	D	X	X			H, X				yellow					green bark
Cercidium microphyllum Foothill palo verde	D	X	X			H, X				yellow				X	green bark
Cercidium praecox Palo brea	S		X			H, X				yellow				X	green bark
Chilopsis linearis Desert willow	D	X	X			H, X	N			pinkish rose	pinkish rose				
Dalbergia sissoo Sissoo	E/S			X											bright green foliage
Leucaena retusa Golden ball lead	D		X				N			gold	gold				papery seed pods
Lysiloma watsonii thornberi Desert fern	E		X			X	L			cream	cream				feathery foliage

118

TREES — Botanical Name / Common Name	Energy Efficiency — Shade	Windbreak	Water Use — Low	Med	High	Wildlife Habitat — Birds	Butterflies	Edible	Fragrant	Spring Color	Summer Color	Fall Color	Winter Color	Thorns	Miscellaneous
Olneya tesota — Ironwood	E	X	X			X		seeds		pinkish purple				X	
Pistachia chinensis — Chinese pistache	D			X								foliage			
Pithecellobium flexicaule — Texas ebony	E	X	X			X			flowers	cream				X	dark green foliage
Pithecellobium mexicanum — Mexican ebony	D	X	X			X				cream				X	
Pithecellobium pallens — Tenaza	E		X						flowers	white	white				
Prosopis glandulosa — Honey mesquite	D		X			X	L, N	seed pods						X	allergen
Prosopis pubescens — Screwbean mesquite	D		X			X								X	allergen, coiled seedpods
Prosopis velutina — Velvet mesquite	D		X			X	L, N	seed pods						X	allergen, shaggy bark
Punica granatum — Pomegranate	D	X	X	X		X		fruit		red		foliage			
Sambucus mexicana — Mexican elderberry	D	X	X			X		berries		cream	cream				
Sophora secundiflora — Texas mountain laurel	E		X						flowers	purple					smells like grape soda
Vitex agnus-castus — Monk's pepper tree	D			X		H	N		flowers	blue pink	blue pink				
Citrus (various)	E				X	X	L, N	fruit	flowers	white					needs fertilizer
Deciduous fruit (various)	D				X	X		fruit	flowers	white pink		foliage			needs fertilizer

SHRUBS Botanical Name / Common Name	Energy Efficiency Shade	Wind-break	Water Use Low	Med	High	Wildlife Habitat Birds	Butter-flies	Edible	Other Characteristics Fragrant	Spring Color	Summer Color	Fall Color	Winter Color	Thorns	Miscellaneous
Abutilon palmeri Superstition mallow			X	X		X				pale orange	pale orange	pale orange			velvety foliage
Acacia greggii Catclaw	D	X	X			X	N		flowers	creamy yellow				X	
Aloysia wrightii Bee bush			X			X			flowers	white				X	
Anisacanthus quadrifidus Desert honeysuckle	D		X	X		H, X	N				orangy red	orangy red			
Atriplex canescens Four-wing saltbush		X	X			X									allergen, fire resistant
Atriplex lentiformis Quailbush		X	X			X									allergen
Berberis haematocarpa Red barberry	E		X			X		berries	flowers	yellow	berries	berries		X	holly-like foliage
Buddleia marrubifolia Wooly butterfly bush			X				N				orange	orange			unusual ball-shaped flowers
Caesalpinia mexicana Mexican bird of paradise			X								yellow	yellow			poisonous seeds
Caesalpinia pulcherrima Red bird of paradise			X				N				orangy red	orangy red			poisonous seeds
Calliandra californica Baja red fairy duster	E		X			H, X	L, N			red	red	red	red		extended bloom
Calliandra eriophylla Pink fairy duster			X			H, X	N			pink			pink		
Celtis pallida Desert hackberry	E	X	X			X	L	berries				berries		X	
Cordia parvifolia Littleleaf cordia	E/S		X				N			white	white	white			

SHRUBS Botanical Name Common Name	Energy Efficiency Shade	Energy Efficiency Wind-break	Water Use Low	Water Use Med	Water Use High	Wildlife Habitat Birds	Wildlife Habitat Butterflies	Edible	Fragrant	Other Characteristics Spring Color	Summer Color	Fall Color	Winter Color	Thorns	Miscellaneous
Dalea frutescens Black dalea			X				L, N					purple	purple		
Dalea pulchra Bush dalea			X			X	N			purple			purple		
Encelia farinosa Brittlebush			X			X	N			yellow			yellow		
Feijoa sellowiana Pineapple guava	E			X				fruit, flowers		pinkish		fruits			can be espaliered
Fortunella sp. Kumquat	E			X		X		fruit	flowers	orange fruit			orange fruit		small tree, needs fertilizer
Hamelia patens Firebush	E		X			H, X					scarlet	scarlet, foliage			
Hyptis emoryi Desert lavender			X				N		foliage	lavender					
Justicia californica Chuparosa			X	X		H, X	L, N	flowers		red, yellow	red, yellow	red, yellow	red, yellow		extended bloom season
Justicia candicans Red justicia			X	X		H, X				red	red	red	red		extended bloom season
Justicia spicigera Mexican honeysuckle			X	X		H, X				orange	orange	orange	orange		extended bloom season
Leucophyllum sp. Texas ranger/Texas sage		low	X			X	N				blue, purple				blooms after rain
Lycium fremontii Wolfberry	D		X			X						berries		X	
Ruellia peninsularis Desert ruellia			X			X				purple	purple	purple	purple		extended bloom season
Salvia clevelandii Chaparral sage			X			X	N		foliage	blue					

121

SHRUBS — Botanical Name / Common Name	Energy Efficiency: Shade	Wind-break	Water Use: Low	Med	High	Wildlife Habitat: Birds	Butter-flies	Edible	Fragrant	Other Characteristics: Spring Color	Summer Color	Fall Color	Winter Color	Thorns	Miscellaneous
Senna artemisioides petiolaris — Silver senna			X										yellow		
Senna lindheimeriana — Velvet leaf senna			X			X					yellow				velvety foliage
Simmondsia chinensis — Jojoba	E	X	X			X		seeds							coffee substitute
Tecoma stans — Yellow bells	D		X	X		X				yellow	yellow	yellow			extended bloom season
Tecoma hybrid 'Orange Jubilee'			X	X						orange	orange	orange			extended bloom season
Vauquelinia californica — Arizona rosewood	E	X	X			X				white					oleander hedge substitute
Ziziphus obtusifolia — Gray thorn	D	X	X			X					black fruits			X	
GROUNDCOVERS															
Convolvulus cneorum — Bush morning glory	E		X							white	white	white			silky foliage
Dalea greggii — Trailing indigo bush			X	X			L, N			purple		purple			
Malephora sp. — Iceplant	E		X	X						yellow to red					fire resistant
Oenothera caespitosa — Tufted evening primrose	E		X				N		flowers (light)	white		white			evening gardens
Rosemarinus officinalis 'Prostatus' / Trailing rosemary	E		X				N		foliage	pale blue			pale blue		attracts bees
Verbena sp. — Verbena	E			X			N			purple	purple	purple			bloom varies by species

PERENNIALS Botanical Name / Common Name	Energy Efficiency: Shade	Wind-break	Water Use: Low	Med	High	Wildlife Habitat: Birds	Butterflies	Edible	Fragrant	Other Characteristics: Spring Color	Summer Color	Fall Color	Winter Color	Thorns	Miscellaneous
Asclepias linaria Pineleaf milkweed			X	X			L, N			white	white	white			papery seed pods
Asclepias subulata Desert milkweed			X				L, N			cream	cream	cream			silky seed pods
Baileya multiradiata Desert marigold			X	X		X	N			yellow	yellow	yellow			
Berlandiera lyrata Chocolate flower			X	X			N		flowers	yellow	yellow	yellow			smells like chocolate
Capsicum annuum v. aviculare Chiltepines			X			X		fruit		fruit	fruit				tiny, hot peppers
Cuphea llavea Bat-faced cuphea			X	X		H				scarlet	scarlet				flowers look like bat faces
Cynara scolymus Globe artichoke				X				fruit	flowers	purple				spiky leaves	dried flowers, needs rich soil
Gaillardia sp. Blanketflower			X				N				yellow, orange				reseeds
Hymenoxys acaulis Angelita daisy			X	X		X	N			yellow	yellow	yellow	yellow		extended bloom season
Melampodium leucanthum Blackfoot daisy			X				N			white	white	white			
Penstemon sp. Penstemon			X			H, X	L			reds, pinks	reds, pinks				
Psilostrophe cooperi Paperflower			X			X	N			yellow	yellow	yellow			dried arrangements
Ratibida columnaris Mexican hat			X							reds, yellows	reds, yellows	reds, yellows			hat-shaped flowers
Salvia coccinea Cherry sage				X		H			foliage	red	red	red			

PERENNIALS	Energy Efficiency		Water Use			Wildlife Habitat		Edible	Other Characteristics							
Botanical Name / Common Name	Shade	Wind-break	Low	Med	High	Birds	Butter-flies		Fragrant	Spring Color	Summer Color	Fall Color	Winter Color	Thorns	Miscellaneous
Salvia leucantha Mexican bush sage				X		H	N		foliage	purple		purple			velvety flowers
Sphaeralcea ambigua Globe mallow			X			X	L, N			many colors					
Tagetes lemonii Mount lemmon marigold			X	X			N	foliage, flowers	foliage, flowers	yellow	yellow		yellow		
Tagetes lucida Mexican tarragon			X	X			N	foliage, flowers	foliage, flowers			yellow			tarragon substitute
ANNUALS															
Dyssodia pentachaeta Golden fleece/Golden dyssodia			X	X			L, N		foliage	gold		gold			can be used as groundcover
Erigeron divergens Spreading fleabane			X	X			N				whitish				reseeds
Eschscholtzia mexicana Mexican gold poppy			X							gold					reseeds
Kallstroemia grandiflora Arizona poppy			X	X							gold				reseeds
Linaria macroccana Toadflax			X							many colors					reseeds
Linum grandiflorum 'Rubrum' Red flax			X	X						red					reseeds
Lupinus sparsiflorus Desert lupine			X	X						purple					reseeds
Orthocarpus purpurascens Owl's clover			X							rosy pink					
Proboscidea sp. Devil's claw			X			X		fruit, seeds			white, pink				basket fibers, reseeds

VINES

Botanical Name / Common Name	Energy Efficiency: Shade	Energy Efficiency: Wind-break	Water Use: Low	Water Use: Med	Water Use: High	Wildlife Habitat: Birds	Wildlife Habitat: Butterflies	Edible	Other Characteristics: Fragrant	Spring Color	Summer Color	Fall Color	Winter Color	Thorns	Miscellaneous
Antigonon leptopus / Coral vine/Queen's wreath	D		X	X							coral	coral			climbs support
Cissus trifoliata / Arizona grape ivy	E		X												climbs support, poisonous tuber
Hardenbergia violacea / Lilac vine	E			X					flowers	purple					climbs support
Lagenaria siceraria / Bottle and dipper gourds	D			X	X		moths			white	white	gourds			climbs support, groundcover
Luffa cylindrica / Luffa	D			X	X		moths			yellow	yellow	gourds			climbs support, luffa sponges
Macfadyena unguis-cati / Cat's claw	E		X							yellow					clings without support
Mascagnia macroptera / Yellow orchid vine	E		X	X						yellow	yellow	papery fruits			climbs support
Maurandya antirrhiniflora / Snapdragon vine	D		X	X						blue, red	blue, red	blue, red			climbs support
Merremia aurea / Yuca vine	E		X								yellow				climbs support
Passiflora foetida / Passion vine	E			X			L	fruit		whitish purple					climbs support
Podranea ricasoliana / Pink trumpet	E		X	X		H				pink	pink	pink			tie to support
Rosa banksiae / Lady Bank's rose	E			X						white, yellow					tie to support, needs fertilizer
Vigna caracalla / Snail vine	D			X						lilac	lilac				climbs support
Vitis sp. / Grapevine	D			X	X	X		fruit							climbs support, pest problems

125

ACCENTS — Botanical Name / Common Name	Energy Efficiency: Shade	Wind-break	Water Use: Low	Med	High	Wildlife Habitat: Birds	Butterflies	Edible	Fragrant	Spring Color	Summer Color	Fall Color	Winter Color	Thorny Spiky	Miscellaneous
Agave macroacantha / Black-spined agave			X											X	bluish leaves with dark spines
Agave vilmoriniana / Octupus agave		low	X												spineless arching leaves
Aloe barbadensis / Aloe vera			X			H				yellow			yellow		gel used as skin salve
Aloe ferox / Cape aloe			X			H				red-orange			red-orange	X	trunk-like stem
Aloe striata / Coral aloe			X			H				coral			coral		pink margins on leaves
Aloe variegata / Partridge breast aloe			X			H				pale orange			pale orange		speckled foliage
Bulbine frutescens / Bulbine			X			H				yellow, orange			yellow, orange		takes shade
Euphorbia antisyphilitica / Candelilla			X												milky sap is poisonous
Fouquieria splendens / Ocotillo			X			H				red				X	
Muhlenbergia capillaris / Pink muhly		low	X	X								pinkish			plumes look great backlit
Muhlenbergia lindheimeri		low	X	X								pale yellow			plumes look great backlit
Opuntia santa rita / Purple prickly pear		low	X			X		fruit		yellow	fruit		purple pads	X	purple deepens when cold
Pedilanthus macrocarpus / Slipper plant			X			H				red-orange		red-orange			
Yucca baccata / Banana yucca		X	X			X		fruit		cream	cream			X	dense flower clusters

Resources

Chapter 1

Permaculture

Earth User's Guide to Permaculture. Rosemary Morrow, 1993. Kangaroo Press, Australia. 0-86417-514-0.

"The Journey Home." Stephanie Mills, 1997. *Sierra Magazine,* (Sept/Oct): 45.

Living Community: A Permaculture Case Study at Sol Y Sombra. Ben Haggard, 1993. Johnson Publishing, Santa Fe.

Living Together: A Permaculture Site Assessment for the Phoenix Zoo Children's Farm. Phoenix Permaculture Team, 1997. Unpublished paper.

Permaculture: A Designer's Manual. Bill Mollison, 1988. Tagari Publications, Tazmania. 0-908228-01-5.

Permaculture: A Practical Guide to a Sustainable Future. Bill Mollison, 1990. Island Press, Washington.

The Permaculture Garden. Graham Bell, 1994. Thorsons, Great Britain. 0-7225-2783-7.

Water for Every Farm. Ken B. Yeomans, 1993. Griffin Press, Australia. 0-646-12954-6.

Rainwater Harvesting

Harvesting Rainwater for Landscape Use. Patricia H. Waterfall, 1998. University of Arizona Cooperative Extension/Low 4 Program. www.ag.arizona.edu/pubs/pubsindex.html#Gardening.

"Harvesting Rain Water Runoff on Your Property." Kirk R. Vincent and Laurie Wirt, 1994. *Permaculture Drylands Journal,* 20 (Aug): 20.

Rainwater Harvesting for Drylands. Brad Lancaster, Rainsource Press, Tucson. www.harvestingrainwater.com/index.html.

Chapter 2

Graywater

Create an Oasis with Greywater: Your Complete Guide to Choosing, Building and Using Greywater. Art Ludwig, 2000, 4th edition. Oasis Design. 0-9643433-0-4. Website contains detailed information on common design mistakes and a chart listing benefits and drawbacks for a wide variety of systems. www.oasisdesign.net/.

The Effect of Graywater on the Growth and Performance of Selected Ornamental Desert Species. César Mazier, 1999. Study conducted at Desert Botanical Garden's Desert House. Available for review at DBG Library, Phoenix.

Graywater Guidelines. Val L. Little, 2001. Water Conservation Alliance of Southern Arizona (Water CASA): Tucson. Available online at www.watercasa.org.

Arizona Department of Environmental Quality, 3033 North Central Ave., Phoenix, 85012, 800-234-5677 to request a copy of graywater regulations. Website contains statewide contact information. www.adeq.state.az.us/index.html.

Drip Irrigation

Guidelines for Drip Irrigation Systems. A technical handbook from the Arizona Landscape Irrigation Guidelines Committee. www.amwua.org/xscp-dripirrigguidelines.htm.

Landscape Watering by the Numbers: A Guide for the Arizona Desert. Donna DiFrancesco and Robyn Baker, 2001. Free publication from Arizona Municipal Water Users Association. Available from Phoenix-area city water conservation offices, or contact AMWUA at 602-248-8482. www.amwua.org.

Xeriscape: Landscaping with Style in the Arizona Desert. A step-by-step guide for planning, installing, and caring for your landscape. Free publication from Arizona Municipal Water Users Association that explains in simple terms how to install a complete drip system. Available from Phoenix-area city water conservation offices, or contact AMWUA at 602-248-8482. www.amwua.org.

Fire

Arizona Firewise Communities. Wide variety of information including fireproofing homes and landscapes, determining your fire risk, and surviving a fire. www.ag.arizona.edu/extension/firewise/.

Arizona Forest Health. Links to many wildfire sites. www.ag.arizona.edu/extension/fh/wildfires.html.

Arizona Interagency Fire Prevention & Education Group. Provides current fire danger alerts, restrictions, and closures. www.azfireinfo.com/.

Creating Wildfire-Defensible Space For Your Home and Property. www.ag.arizona.edu/pubs/natresources/az1290/.

Firewise. Site sponsored by the National Wildland/Urban Interface Fire Program containing information for people who live in fire-prone areas. www.firewise.org/.

Firewise Plant Materials for 3,000 ft. and Higher Elevations. List of trees, shrubs, and grasses. www.ag.arizona.edu/pubs/natresources/az1289.html.

Fire-Resistant Landscaping. www.ag.arizona.edu/pubs/natresources/az1291/.

USDA Forest Service, Southwestern Region, 333 Broadway SE, Albuquerque, NM 87102, 505-842-3292. Wide variety of information on wildfires, natural resources, wildlife, and conservation efforts. Includes index of free video-lending library. www.fs.fed.us/r3/.

Chapter 3

<u>Wildlife Habitat</u>

Coexisting with Urban Wildlife, A Guide to the Central Arizona Uplands. Robert L. Hoffa, 1996. Sharlot Hall Museum Press, Prescott, AZ. 0-927579-07-3.

Desert Bird Gardening, 1997. Arizona Native Plant Society, P.O. Box 41206, Sun Station, Tucson, AZ 85717. http://aznps.org.

Desert Butterfly Gardening, 1996. Arizona Native Plant Society, P.O. Box 41206, Sun Station, Tucson, AZ 85717. http://aznps.org.

Desert Hummingbird Gardens. Sylvia Yoder, 1999. Real Estate Consulting and Education, Inc., Paradise Valley, AZ. 0-9669060-3-9.

Efficacy and Methodology of Urban Pigeon Control. Keith M. Blanton, et al. http://wildlifedamage.unl.edu/handbook/Chapters/pdf/fech13.pdf.

Gardening for Pollinators. Mrill Ingram, Stephen Buchmann, and Gary Nabhan, 1998. Arizona Sonora Desert Museum Press, 2021 N. Kinney Road, Tucson, 85743. 1-886679-10-X.

Landscaping for Desert Wildlife. Carolyn Engel-Wilson, 1999, 2nd ed. Available at Arizona Game & Fish Department, 2221 West Greenway Road, Phoenix, 85023, 602-942-3000, or 7200 E. University, Mesa, 85207, 480-981-9400.

Pests. Information on controlling unwanted vertebrate pests from the Arizona Master Gardener Manual online. www.ag.arizona.edu/pubs/garden/mg/pests/intro.html#vertebrate.

70 Common Butterflies of the Southwest. Richard Bailowitz & Douglas Danforth, 1997. Southwest Parks and Monuments Association, Tucson.

Arizona Game & Fish Department, 2221 W. Greenway Road, Phoenix, 85023, 602-942-3000. Regional Offices: Region I, Box 57201, Pinetop, 85935, 928-367-4281. Region II, 3500 S. Lake Mary Rd., Flagstaff, 86001, 928-774-5045. Region III, 5325 N. Stockton Hill Rd., Kingman, 86401, 928-692-7700. Region IV, 9140 E. County 10-1/2 St., Yuma, 85365, 928-342-0091. Region V, 555 N. Greasewood Rd., Tucson, 85745, 520-628-5376. Region VI, 7200 E. University, Mesa, 85207, 480-981-9400. www.gf.state.az.us.

Arizona Herpetological Association, P.O. Box 64531, Phoenix, AZ 85082-4531, 480-894-1625. Contains photos of snakes and lizards commonly found in Arizona. Volunteers will remove snakes from homes and yards. www.azreptiles.com.

Bat Conservation International, P.O. Box 162603, Austin, TX 78716, 512-327-9721. www.batcon.org.

California Department of Fish and Game, 1416 Ninth St., Sacramento, CA 95814, 916445-0411. www.dfg.ca.gov/dfghome.html.

New Mexico Department of Game & Fish, P. O. Box 25112, Santa Fe, NM 87504, 800-862-9310. www.gmfsh.state.nm.us/.

Organization for Bat Conservation, 39221 Woodward Ave., Bloomfield, MI 48303, 248-645-3232. www.batconservation.org/.

Project FeederWatch and Classroom FeederWatch, Cornell Lab of Ornithology, 159 Sapsucker Woods Road, Ithaca, NY 14850, 800-843-2473. Help scientists study bird populations by counting the visitors at your feeders. www.birds.cornell.edu.

Sonoran Arthropod Studies Institute, P.O. Box 5624, Tucson, AZ 85703-0624, 520-883-3945. www.sasionline.org/.

Southeast Arizona Butterfly Association meets monthly at the Tucson Botanical Gardens, 2150 N. Alvernon Way. www.naba.org/chapters/nabasa/home.html.

Southwestern Herpetologists Society, P.O. Box 7469, Van Nuys, CA 91409-7469, 818-503-2052. www.swhs.org.

Texas Parks & Wildlife, 4200 Smith School Road, Austin, TX 78744, 800-792-1112, 512-389-4800. www.tpwd.state.tx.us/.

Thousand Friends of Frogs, Center for Global Environmental Education, Hamline University Graduate School of Education, 1536 Hewitt Avenue, St. Paul, MN 55104-1284, 651-523-2945. www.cgee.hamline.edu/frogs/index.htm.

Tucson Audubon Society, 300 E. University, #120, Tucson, AZ 85705, 520-629-0510. www.tucsonaudubon.org/.

Urban Wildlife Sanctuary Program, The Humane Society of the U.S., 2100 L Street NW, Washington, DC 20037, 202-452-1100. www.hsus.org/.

<u>Edible Landscapes</u>

Citrus: Complete Guide to Selecting & Growing More than 100 Varieties, Lance Walheim, 1996. Ironwood Press, Tucson. 0-9628236-4-3.

The Complete Book of Edible Landscaping, Rosalind Creasy, 1982. Sierra Club Books. 087156-249-9.

Desert Gardening for Beginners: How to Grow Vegetables, Flowers and Herbs in an Arid Climate. Cathy Cromell, Linda A. Guy & Lucy K. Bradley, 1999. Arizona Master Gardener Press, Phoenix. 0-9651987-2-3. Soil improvement, growing seasons, watering, fertilizing, and planting calendars.

Edible Flowers: From Garden to Palate. Cathy Wilkinson Barash, 1993. Fulcrum Publishing. 1-55591-164-1.

Low Desert Citrus Varieties. Michael Mauer and Lucy K. Bradley, 1998. University of Arizona Cooperative Extension. www.ag.arizona.edu/pubs/pubsindex.html#Gardening.

The Low Desert Herb Gardening Handbook. Arizona Herb Association, 1997, azherb1@home.com, 602-470-8086, ext. 830.

Native Seeds/SEARCH, 526 N. 4th Ave., Tucson, AZ 85705-8450, 520-622-5561. Plants traditionally grown by Native Americans in the Southwest. Emphasis on corn, beans, squash, and chilies as well as more unusual crops, such as devil's claw, sorghum, tomatillo, chiltepines, cotton, and indigo. www.nativeseeds.org.

Seeds of Change, P.O. Box 15700, Santa Fe, NM 87592-1500, 888-762-7333. Organically grown vegetable, flower, and herb seeds. www.store.yahoo.com/seedsofchange/.

Seeds West Garden Seeds, 317 14th St. NW, Albuquerque, NM 87104, 505-843-9713. Flowers, vegetables, and herbs for the Southwest. www.seedswestgardenseeds.com.

Low-Allergen Gardening

Allergy-Free Gardening: The Revolutionary Guide to Healthy Landscaping. Thomas Leo Ogren, 2000. Ten Speed Press, Berkeley. 1-58008-166-5.

Pollen.com. Pollen forecasts by U.S. zipcode and information on pollens and allergies. www.pollen.com/.

Native and Desert-Adapted Plants

Agaves, Yuccas, and Related Plants: A Gardener's Guide. Gary Irish & Mary Irish, 2000. Timber Press, Portland. 0-8819244-2-3.

Desert Accent Plants, 1992. Arizona Native Plant Society, P.O. Box 41206, Sun Station, Tucson, AZ 85717. http://aznps.org.

Desert Grasses, 1993. Arizona Native Plant Society, P.O. Box 41206, Sun Station, Tucson, AZ 85717. http://aznps.org.

Desert Groundcovers and Vines, 1991. Arizona Native Plant Society, P.O. Box 41206, Sun Station, Tucson, AZ 85717. http://aznps.org.

Desert Landscaping for Beginners. Lucy Bradley, et al.,

2001. Arizona Master Gardener Press, Phoenix. 0-9651987-3-1.

Desert Shrubs, 1990. Arizona Native Plant Society, P.O. Box 41206, Sun Station, Tucson, AZ 85717. http://aznps.org.

Desert Trees, 1990. Arizona Native Plant Society, P.O. Box 41206, Sun Station, Tucson, AZ 85717. http://aznps.org.

Gardening in the Desert. Mary F. Irish, 2000. The University of Arizona Press, Tucson. 0-8165-2057-7.

Landscape Plants for Dry Regions. Warren Jones and Charles Sacamano, 2000. Fisher Books, Tucson. 1-55561-190-7.

Low Water Use Plants for California and the Southwest. Carol Schuler, 1993. Fisher Books, Tucson. 1-55561-271-7.

Native Plants for Southwestern Deserts. Judy Mielke, 1993. University of Texas Press, Austin. 0-292-75147-8.

Natural by Design: Beauty and Balance in Southwest Gardens. Judith Phillips, 1995. Museum of New Mexico Press, Santa Fe. 0-89013-227-1.

Plant Selection and Selecting Your Plants. Elizabeth Davison, John Begeman, Jimmy L. Tipton, 2000. University of Arizona Cooperative Extension, Tucson. Publication AZ1153.

Plants for Dry Climates: How to Select, Grow and Enjoy. Mary Rose Duffield and Warren D. Jones, 2000. Fisher Books, Tucson. 1-55561-270-9.

Lady Bird Johnson Wildflower Center provides links to native plant organizations in North America and "Factpacts" that contain lists of native plants by region and sources for plants and seeds. www.wildflower.org.

Wild Seed, Inc., P.O. Box 27751, Tempe, AZ 85285, 602-276-3536. Request a free catalog for native seed material.

Places to see native and desert-adapted plants in Arizona

Cochise County

Bisbee. Arizona Cactus Botanical Garden, 8 South Cactus Lane. www.arizonacactus.com/.

Sierra Vista. Plant Sciences Center, The University of Arizona South Campus, 1140 N.Colombo. www.ag.arizona.edu/cochise/psc.

Sierra Vista. Sara Gibbs Botanical Garden, behind Public Library, 2600 E. Tacoma, Sierra Vista.

Coconino County

Flagstaff Arboretum, off Route 66 on Woody Mountain Road. www.thearb.org/.

Flagstaff. Northern Arizona University, entire campus. Open 24 hours, 7 days a week for self-guided viewing. www.nau.edu.

La Paz County

Lake Havasu City. Lake Havasu State Park, 699 London Bridge Rd. www.pr.state.az.us/parkhtml/havasu.html.

Maricopa County

Chandler. Xeriscape Demonstration Garden, NW corner of Erie St. and Arrowhead Dr.

Chandler. Hummingbird Habitat, SW corner of Desert Breeze Park, between Ray and Chandler & Rural and McLintock Rds.

Gilbert. Riparian Preserve at Water Ranch, SE corner of Guadalupe and Greenfield, next to the Southeast Regional Library.

Gilbert. Wildlife Habitat Facility, behind Fire Station on E. side of Cooper Rd. between Guadalupe and Elliot Rds.

Glendale. Elsie McCarthy Sensory Garden. www.ci.glendale.az.us/Recreation/Elsie-McCarthySensory-Garden.cfm.

Glendale. Xeriscape Botanical Garden, Glendale Public Library, 5959 W. Brown Street, 59th Ave. just S. of Peoria Ave. www.ci.glendale.az.us/WaterConservation/xeriscapegarden.cfm.

Mesa. Desert Botanical Walk, Superstition Springs Center Mall, Superstition Freeway and Power Rd.

Mesa Xeriscape Demonstration Garden, Mesa Community College, Dobson Road just N. of Superstition Freeway.

Phoenix. Desert Botanical Garden, 1201 N. Galvin Pkwy. www.dbg.org.

Phoenix. Master Gardener Demonstration Garden and Landscape Trail, Maricopa County Cooperative Extension, 4341 E. Broadway Rd. www.ag.arizona.edu/maricopa/garden/.

Tempe. Arizona State University Arboretum, entire campus. Open 24 hours, 7 days a week for self-guided viewing. www.fm.asu.edu/arboretum.htm.

Tempe Xeriscape Demonstration Gardens, Tempe Public Library, SW corner of Rural and Southern Avenues & Tempe Woman's Club Park, NE corner of Weber Dr. and College Ave.

Pima County

Sahuarita. Master Gardener Demonstration Garden, Pima County Cooperative Extension Satellite Office, 18050 S. La Canada Rd. www.ag.arizona.edu/pima/gardening/.

Tucson. Arizona-Sonora Desert Museum. 2021 N. Kinney Rd. http://desertmuseum.org/visit/planning.html.

Tucson. Master Gardener "Our Yard" Landscape Learning Center, Pima County Cooperative Extension, 4210 N. Campbell Ave. www.//ag.arizona.edu/pima/gardening/.

Tucson. Tohono Chul Park, 7366 N. Paseo del Norte. www.tohonochulpark.org.

Tucson. University of Arizona, entire campus. Open 24 hours, 7 days a week for self-guided viewing. www.ag.arizona.edu/arboretum/.

Tucson Botanical Garden, 2150 N. Alvernon Way, SE of Grant & Alvernon. www.tucsonbotanical.org/.

Pinal County

Superior. Boyce Thompson Arboretum, 37615 Highway 60. www.ag.arizona.edu/BTA/.

Chapter 4

Watering

Arizona Drought Resources. Links to various sites related to water management. www.ag.arizona.edu/extension/temp/drought.

Handbook of Water Use and Conservation. Amy Vickers, 2001. Water Plow Press, Amherst, MA. 1-931579-07-5.

Landscape Watering by the Numbers: A Guide for the Arizona Desert. Donna DiFrancesco and Robyn Baker, 2001. Free publication from Arizona Municipal Water Users Association. Available from Phoenix-area city water conservation offices, or contact AMWUA at 602-248-8482. www.amwua.org.

Save: The Homeowner's Guide to Using Water Wisely. Tucson Water, 1994.

Water Use It Wisely. Tips for saving water in the home and landscape. www.wateruseitwisely.com.

Water: A practical guide to using and conserving water in the garden. Susan McClure, 2000. Workman Publishing, New York. 0-7611-1778-4.

Arizona Municipal Water Users Association, 4041 North Central Avenue, Suite 900, Phoenix, 85012, 602-248-8482. AMWUA is a non-profit organization established by the cities of Chandler, Gilbert, Glendale, Goodyear, Mesa, Peoria, Phoenix, Scottsdale, and Tempe for the development of an urban water policy. They provide a wide range of information on conserving water in the home and landscape. www.amwua.org.

Low 4 Program, University of Arizona Pima County Cooperative Extension, 520-622-7701. Free workshops on water conservation, xeriscape and rainwater harvesting. Separate sessions designed for homeowners and landscape industry. www.ag.arizona.edu/pima/low4/index.html.

Maricopa County Vector Control. Provides information on controlling mosquitoes, which breed in shallow water. www.maricopa.gov/envsvc/WATER/VECTOR/veccntrl.htm.

Project WET (Water Education for Teachers) provides teaching aids for kindergarteners through 12th graders. A Non-point Source Water Pollution Curriculum for grades 9-12 is also available. www.ag.arizona.edu/AZWATER/wet/index.html.

Water Conservation Alliance of Arizona (Water CASA). Provides information on saving water in the home and landscape. www.watercasa.org/.

Water Resources Research Center, College of Agriculture and Life Sciences, The University of Arizona, 350 N. Campbell Ave., Tucson, AZ 85721, 520-792-9591. Coordinates university research at all three Arizona universities on state and regional water issues and provides research information to interested parties. www.ag.arizona.edu/AZWATER/main.html.

Water Wise, University of Arizona Cochise County Cooperative Extension, Sierra Vista, 520-458-8278, ext. 2141. Community education program for Cochise County on a variety of water-saving topics, including rainwater harvesting. www.ag.arizona.edu/cochise/waterwise.

Mulching, Composting, and Fertilizing

Backyard Composting: Your Complete Guide to Recycling Yard Clippings. Harmonious Technologies, 1992. Harmonius Press, Ojai, CA. 0-9629768-0-6.

Chemical-Free Yard & Garden: The Ultimate Authority on Successful Organic Gardening. Anna Carr, et al., 1991. Rodale Press, Emmaus, PA. 0-87857-951-6.

Desert Landscaping for Beginners. Lucy Bradley, et al., 2001. Arizona Master Gardener Press, Phoenix. 0-09651987-3-1. Chapter on maintaining healthy desert turf, including mowing to leave clippings on the lawn. Specific fertilizing recommendations for citrus, roses, cacti, and turf.

Let It Rot! The Gardener's Guide to Composting. Stu Campbell, 1990. Storey Communications, Pownal, VT.

Worms Eat My Garbage. Mary Appelhof, 1997. Flower Press, Kalamazoo, MI. 0942256-10-7.

Arizona Department of Environmental Quality Main Office, 1110 W. Washington St., Phoenix, 85007, 602-771-2300. Northern Regional Office, 1515 E. Cedar Ave., Suite F, Flagstaff, 86004, 928-779-0313. Southern Regional Office, 400 W. Congress, Suite 433, Tucson, 85701, 520-628-6733. Toll Free in AZ 800-234-5677. Promotes "Reduce, Recycle, Reuse" through a variety of programs, educational outreach, and funding opportunities. www.adeq.state.az.us/.

Sierra Vista Compost Facility, E. Hwy 90 (mile post 325), Sierra Vista, AZ 520-458-7530. Public drops off yard trimmings and receives free compost.

Tucson Organic Gardeners, P.O. Box 27763, Tucson, AZ 85726, 520-670-9158. Promotes organic gardening, including composting and mulching, through workshops, events, and garden tours. www.iwhome.com/nonprofits/TOG/.

U.S. Environmental Protection Agency. Provides information, program assistance, and research results on a wide variety of issues, as well as resources geared to children. www.epa.gov.

Links to numerous composting sites: www.oldgrowth.org/compost/home.

Links to resources on composting for all states: www.mastercomposter.com/.

Pruning

Desert Landscaping for Beginners. Lucy K. Bradley, et al., 2001. Arizona Master Gardener Press, Phoenix. 0-9651987-3-1. Describes how and when to prune different types of plants.

How to Prune Young Shade Trees. Tree City USA Bulletin #1. National Arbor Day Foundation. www.arborday.org/programs/treecitybulletins.html.

Pruning, Planting & Care. Eric A. Johnson, 1997. Ironwood Press, Tucson. 0-96282361.

American Society of Consulting Arborists, 15245 Shady Grove Road, Suite 130, Rockville, MD 20850, 301-947-0483. Membership is for arborists who specialize in advising, diagnosing, recommending treatments, making appraisals, and offering legal testimony. Website contains a list of members by state and specialty. www.asca-consultants.org.

Arizona Community Tree Council, Inc., 1616 W. Adams, Phoenix, AZ 85007, 602-542-6191. A non-profit organization that promotes communication and the exchange of information about trees, and the essential role they play in the well-being of all Arizona communities. Encourages and facilitates the planting and care of trees throughout the state. Website contains links to many tree-related sites. http://aztrees.org/.

International Society of Arboriculture (ISA), P.O. Box 3129, Champaign, IL 61826-3129, 217-355-9411. ISA offers two levels of certification: Certified Arborist and Certified Tree Worker. Certification requires knowledge of tree biology, species identification and selection, soils and tree nutrition, planting, pruning, cabling, bracing, and problem diagnosis. It also requires 18 months of experience in Arboriculture and 30 hours of continuing education every three years. Enter your zip code at the website and obtain a list of certified arborists in your area. www.isa-arbor.com/arborists/arborist.html.

National Arborist Association, 3 Perimeter Road, Unit 1, Manchester NH 03103, 800-733-2622. Membership is commercial tree care service firms with standards for pruning, cabling, and other techniques. www.natlarb.com.

Chapter 5

Insects and Integrated Pest Management

Corn Gluten Meal Research Site. Information on corn gluten meal as a natural herbicide. www.gluten.iastate.edu/home.html.

Environmentally Responsible Gardening & Landscaping in the Low Desert. Maricopa County Cooperative Extension website contains information to help diagnosis plant problems. www.ag.arizona.edu/maricopa/garden/.

Home Landscaping Guide for Lake Tahoe and Vicinity. John Cobourn, et al. University of Nevada, Reno Cooperative Extension.

An Illustrated Guide to Arizona Weeds. Kittie F. Parker, 1990. University of Arizona Press, Tucson. 0-8165-0288-9. www.uapress.arizona.edu/online.bks/weeds titlweed.htm.

Insects of the Southwest. Floyd Werner & Carl Olson, 1994. Fisher Books, Tucson, 155561-060-9.

In A Desert Garden: Love and Death Among the Insects. John Alcock, 1997. The University of Arizona Press, Tucson, 0-8165-1970-6.

IPM in Practice: Principles and Methods of Integrated Pest Management. Mary Lou Flint and P. Gouveia, 2001. University of California ANR Publication 3418. 1-879906-50-3.

IPM in Schools. Dawn Gouge, et al. University of Arizona College of Agriculture and Life Sciences, Tucson. www.ag.arizona.edu/pubs/insects/az1234.pdf.

Master Gardener Entomology Manual. Dave T. Langston and Roberta Gibson, 1995. The University of Arizona College of Agriculture and Life Sciences, Tucson. Order from http://ag.arizona.edu/pubs/.

Natural Enemies Handbook: The Illustrated Guide to Biological Pest Control. Mary Lou Flint and S.H. Dreistadt, 1998. University of California ANR Publication 3389. 1-879906-41-4.

Natural Gardening. John Kadel Boring, et al., 1995. The Nature Company/Time-Life Books. 0-7835-4750-1.

Pests & Diseases: The Complete Guide to Preventing, Identifying, and Treating Plant Problems. Pippa Greenwood, et al., 2000. Dorling Kindersley, NY. 0-7894-5074-7.

Pests of Landscape Trees and Shrubs: An Integrated Pest Management Guide. S. H. Dreistadt, 1994. University of California ANR Publication 3359. 1-879906-18-X.

Pests of the Garden and Small Farm: A Grower's Guide to Using Less Pesticide. Mary Louise Flint, 1998 2nd ed. University of California Press, Berkeley. 0-520-21810-8.

Pests of the West: Prevention and Control for Today's Garden and Small Farm. Whitney Cranshaw, 1998. Fulcrum Publishing, Golden, CO. 1-55591-401-2.

Tree of Life Jumping Spiders. Photos of jumping spiders. www.tolweb.org/tree/phylogeny.html.

UC IPM Online. Wide variety of IPM information from the University of California, including management strategies for pests and weeds. www.ipm.ucdavis.edu/.

What's Bugging You in Arizona? Photos and information on bugs, vertebrates, diseases, weeds, and beneficial insects. www.ag.arizona.edu/urbanipm.

University of Arizona County Cooperative Extension County Offices

http://ag.arizona.edu/apache/

http://ag.arizona.edu/cochise/

http://ag.arizona.edu/coconino/

http://ag.arizona.edu/gila/

http://ag.arizona.edu/graham/

http://ag.arizona.edu/greenlee/

http://ag.arizona.edu/lapaz/

http://ag.arizona.edu/maricopa/

http://ag.arizona.edu/mohave/

http://ag.arizona.edu/navajo/

http://ag.arizona.edu/pima/

http://ag.arizona.edu/pinal/

http://ag.arizona.edu/santacruz/

http://ag.arizona.edu/yavapai/

http://ag.arizona.edu/yuma/ ✳

Bios

Cathy Cromell is an Instructional Specialist in Urban Horticulture with the University of Arizona Maricopa County Cooperative Extension in Phoenix. She manages Arizona Master Gardener Press to publish books and other materials specific to gardening in the Sonoran Desert. She also writes a monthly gardening column for *Phoenix Home & Garden* magazine and a bi-weekly column as southwest regional editor for the National Gardening Association. Cathy is a certified Master Gardener and Master Composter.

Jo Miller is the Water Conservation Coordinator for the City of Glendale. Her experience includes 19 years as owner of a landscape design and maintenance company specializing in permaculture design systems. She has worked with Maricopa County Cooperative Extension and the Arizona Department of Education as a gardening specialist for the USDA Team Nutrition teacher-training to promote children's gardening and nutrition and is a mentor/teacher for Prescott College. In 1997, she completed a design assessment and consultation for the Harmony Farm area at the Phoenix Zoo. Jo has provided volunteer consultation to several school and community garden projects and presents gardening and design workshops to the community. One of her greatest joys in life is pretending she is tending her garden.

Lucy K. Bradley is the Urban Horticulture Agent for the University of Arizona Maricopa County Cooperative Extension in Phoenix. She works with home horticulture, school gardens, community gardens, the Master Gardeners, and other urban gardening programs in the County. Lucy has a Masters degree in Botany from Arizona State University. She is a Certified Arborist and has served on the board of the Arizona Community Tree Council.

Janice Austin has a background as an artist, educator, and avid gardener. With a Master of Fine Arts degree, she is an instructor and coordinator for Arizona State University's Herberger College of Fine Arts, helping students find their niche through internships and career preparation. A recently certified Master Gardener, she has been gardening all her life and illustrating the beauty she finds in nature, using drawing, painting, sculpture, poetry, and prose.

Photo Credits

Lucy K. Bradley, co-author: black widow spider, bumblebee, cicada, cochineal scale on purple prickly pear, black swallowtail on orange flower, praying mantid adult.

Entomologist Roberta Gibson: aphids on milkweed, green lacewing egg, leafcutter bee nests and damage, palm flower caterpillars, tobacco hornworm.

Joanne Littlefield, University of Arizona Cooperative Extension: centipede, grapeleaf skeletonizers.

New Mexico State University: syrphid fly adult.

Sonoran Arthropod Studies Institute, Steve Prchal, photographer: agave weevil, salt marsh caterpillar.

The University of Arizona Cooperative Extension Maricopa Agricultural Center: agave weevil damage, assassin bug, beet leafhopper, cabbage looper adult and damage, carpenter bee nests, cicada skin, cutworm and damage, false chinch bugs (2), fig beetle and larvae, ladybeetle pupae, leafcutter bee, thrips (3), palo verde root borers, praying mantid egg case, psyllid adult, egg, and damage, spider mites and damage, sunspider, tailless whipscorpion, whipscorpion, whiteflies and damage.

The University of California Statewide IPM Program, Jack Kelly Clark, photographer: aphid mummies, crab spider, damsel bug adult and nymph, green lacewing adult, ladybeetle adult and larvae, minute pirate bug, parasitic wasp (2), *Tricogramma* wasp, syrphid fly adult on purple flower and larvae.

The University of Texas Cooperative Extension: assassin bug with bollworm, big-eyed bug, black swallowtail adult and larvae, cabbage looper, cochineal scale, cutworm with seedling, damsel bug, flea beetles, giant swallowtail, green June beetle and larvae, green lacewing larvae, gulf fritillary and caterpillar, monarch butterfly caterpillar, pupae, and adult, oleander aphids, orange dog caterpillar, psyllids, spined soldier bug adult and nymph, spittlebug, white-lined sphinx moth.

Index